A Passion for Travel

A Passion for Travel

New Zealand Writers
& their Adventures Overseas

Edited by Tina Shaw

TANDEM PRESS

First published in New Zealand in 1998 by
TANDEM PRESS
2 Rugby Road, Birkenhead, Auckland 10
New Zealand

Copyright © Introduction and this selection, Tina Shaw, 1998.
Copyright in the individual contributions to this collection remains the property of the individual contributors.
ISBN 1 877178 31 4

All rights reserved. No part of this publication may be reproduced, stored in a retrieval system or transmitted in any form or by any means, electronic, mechanical, photocopying, recording or otherwise without prior written permission of the publishers.

Cover design by Sue Reidy
Production and text design by M & F Whild Typesetting Services, Auckland
Typesetting by Typesetting Services, Auckland
Printed in New Zealand by Publishing Press Limited

Contents

Introduction 1

Letter from Bush Alaska 5
Joy Cowley

History as it Happens 17
CK Stead

Of Bonaparte and Blue Suede Shoes 35
Sarah Quigley

Neighbourhood Wars in Belvoye 49
Lloyd Jones

The Last Time I Saw Paris 69
Joy MacKenzie

Safari 85
Catharina van Bohemen

Grin Like a Dog 101
Peter Wells

Journey to the Interior 113
Graeme Lay

A London Engagement 133
Barbara Else

Safeguarding the Cotton Castles 147
Tessa Duder

Mexican Honeymoon 165
Michaelanne Forster

Eight Days in Antarctica 177
Chris Orsman

Contributors' biographical notes 198

Introduction

WHEN I WAS twelve my father won a large sum of money at the races and our family did a 'world tour'. Coming from the insular world of rural Waikato this was a big deal. I knew no one else who had been further than Fiji. We set off – I imagine rather like the *Beverly Hillbillies* – and saw all the famous things that we had only heard about: Disneyland, Paris, the *Mona Lisa*, the Black Forest, the Danube! The food was bizarre, the people were incomprehensible, taxi drivers were rude. I mostly remember the simple things: pigeons on the stone window-sills of our London hotel; the hundreds of pigeons that thronged the Piazza San Marco in Venice; and the brightly coloured vases that filled the glassblowers' shop windows. It was thrilling to visit countries so different from my own, yet I was very relieved to get back home again.

Travel is a national pastime for New Zealanders (for those who can afford it), practically an obsession. The tiny godwit undertakes a huge journey instinctively – flying nonstop from the Firth of Thames to Siberia – and we too seem to have been born with an instinct to pitch ourselves over the oceans, to all points of the earth, with a sort of cheerful and slightly manic nonchalance, throwing ourselves into overseas adventures with an almost reckless abandon.

This curious trait first manifests itself in our coming-of-age rite, the great OE. Throughout my lifetime young New Zealanders have been going off and making the world their own – putting their stamp on it in some way, whether it's squatting in London or crewing expensive yachts in the Mediterranean. But come middle-age and then retirement, most of us are still heading off overseas, or dreaming of it. Our need to get away doesn't diminish as we get older. If anything, it intensifies.

What drives us to do it? After all, we could stay home and play Scrabble.

At the most basic level there is a desire to experience something more besides the sights and sounds that we are daily accustomed to. If you live on a sparsely populated island you long, eventually, to experience vast plains of tundra, or masses of people you've never seen before in your life. There is a longing for difference. Travel, with its promise of the exotic – foreign currencies, strange languages, odd foods – fills that need.

As Lloyd Jones puts it, 'Somehow, and in spite of ourselves we fall across seas, continents, into each other's arms, surprised at first, then kind of liking the way the foreign bits come round to our touch.'

And foreign places are doubly foreign for us New Zealanders because of the extraordinary effort involved in just getting there. People in Britain have only to hop across the Channel to experience a different culture. We have to travel for hours, days even, to reach a destination. My own direct flight to Heathrow, as an adult, is vividly etched in my mind as a nightmare of narrow seats, plastic food, gritty eyes and continuous-playing *Rocky* sagas. It was awful, but I had to do it – to see, again, what the rest of the world looked like.

Once we arrive, being there can be exhilarating, or terrifying: culture shock is no respecter of persons – even hardy, self-sufficient outdoor types have been known to succumb to the odd panic attack. But on the whole, New Zealanders thrive on challenges, and the challenge of travel is a big part of the attraction. We undertake a big journey, like climbing a mountain because, well, it's there. We want to be a Hillary and 'knock the bastard off'.

We simply can't help ourselves. No more than we can help comparing ourselves to all those alien cultures we travel such distances to bump into. We need to know how we measure up to the rest of the world. Are we really as clever and lucky as we have been led to believe we are? Has anybody over there even heard of us? We need to know. But most important, we need to see and we need to feel the difference. It's all to do with honing our sense of national identity –

Introduction

another national obsession, one we can pursue wholeheartedly only when we travel.

'Over there' is also where many of us, or our forebears, originally hailed from. Where past generations had their roots, where they packed their bags and set off to these rocky isles to start a new life. There is an inborn curiosity that sees many of us making pilgrimages to little villages in Ireland or Britain.

But whatever it is that feeds our obsession with travel – a search for identity, a longing for adventure, simple curiosity, a desperate desire to escape these narrow islands, or some combination of all these things – the recipe has made us passionate travellers.

Peter Wells's passion is for Sydney, a city 'ripe for the millennium', and a place where he can escape the confines of this country. Catharina van Bohemen, on African safari, takes on the challenge of a hostile environment. Experiencing the heady mix of Tahitian and French culture, Graeme Lay heads well off the beaten track.

Michaelanne Forster goes in search of passion, but a second honeymoon in Mexico has unforeseen consequences. Joy Cowley experiences how different life can be in Alaskan villages, where hunting is part of the daily business of survival. A foreign culture is also explored in Lloyd Jones's quest to Brooklyn, a world away from the safe environment back home.

Curiosity compels Sarah Quigley and friends to explore Corsica, where the locals are irreverent about their famous history, while Barbara Else discovers how different a working journey can be from a tourist jaunt when she goes on a book tour in London and Manchester.

CK Stead's initial contact with Croatia is also via writing business, but he returns to explore a country where history can be inherited 'almost as an aspect of personality', and is shocked by a countryside that is both beautiful and scarred. A marriage of two cultures takes Tessa Duder to a small village in Turkey, where she indulges in a passion for silica terraces and hot pools. Joy MacKenzie's Paris is rich with literary culture, and redolent with romance.

The idea of exploration is nowhere stronger than in Chris Orsman's writing about Antarctica, a place that has long held a personal fascination. This is a continent etched with a brittle history: to read about Scott's final base is to visit it oneself, and hear the whisper of ghosts.

Bringing this book together has been a team effort. I am indebted to Stephen Stratford, who has worked with me on this project from its earliest stages, and to Graeme Lay, who has been generous with his advice. And finally I thank the 12 writers who have contributed such unique and compelling stories to this collection. I hope you will be as inspired in reading this anthology as I have been in compiling it.

Tina Shaw
May, 1998

Letter from Bush Alaska

Joy Cowley

A Passion for Travel

IT BEGAN THREE years ago with a letter from Kipi Asipisik, a teacher in the Eskimo village of Shaktoolik, north-west Alaska. She enclosed a two-sentence letter from a six-year-old boy who had begun reading on the early Story Box books. A correspondence developed, then broadened to include other schools in the Bering Strait district, and an invitation to visit these isolated villages where there are no roads and where Yupik and Inupiak peoples live as they have always done, by hunting and fishing and gathering.

The night from New Zealand was a long one – Auckland to Honolulu, to San Francisco, to Seattle, to Anchorage and then to Unalakleet, the biggest village in the school district. About six hundred people live in small wooden houses along a beach near the mouth of a river. Behind the village is the tundra, miles of low-growing vegetation which reaches up to hills whose bald tops have been polished by millions of years of snow and ice.

This far north there is permafrost. About two feet down the earth is rock-hard frozen. It never thaws. The upper two feet, which is thawed for about four months of the year, supports a thick mat of spongy vegetation. My childhood geography lessons had me believe that tundra was lichen that reindeer ate in winter, pawing back the snow to get at it. And yes, there is some lichen in places, a white fibrous lichen like the hairy stuff that grows on our fences and fruit trees back home. And the reindeer herds do eat it in winter. But there is a wide variety of seasonal plant life on tundra, much of which provides food for the people who live in these regions. When the snows melt in late May, there is almost instant growth and flowering. Then, from August through to the end of September, come the berries: first, the blueberries, then the salmonberries which are the colour of salmon flesh, then blackberries (which are the same size and shape as blueberries) and finally the cranberries. All of these grow close to the ground along with an assortment of cotton grass, wild irises and other low-growing plants. The tundra is lumpy and soggy to walk on.

There is no shortage of berries. They grow everywhere, thousands of miles of them, although some places are better for picking than others. Over the summer vacation, families go camping to pick berries, to hunt moose and caribou, and to fish. Twice I was treated to Eskimo ice-cream, which is made with a mixture of reindeer tallow, seal oil, sugar and berries. It's very good too, if you don't mind ice-cream which tastes like cod-liver oil. Other foods I've eaten here have been silver salmon, reindeer steaks, caribou and moose. But I didn't follow up an offer to taste fermented walrus meat which is packed in the earth next to the permafrost and left to ferment slowly over several months. 'Stink meat', the people call it. I guess it's sort of like animal sauerkraut.

I had been told that Eskimo peoples have no vegetables in their diet, but in this area that is not true. Apart from the berries, they get vitamin C from shoots and small tubers which grow in the tundra. These they pickle or freeze for winter.

At this time of the year, the tundra glows with autumn colours, red and yellow with patches of brown; but as the temperature drops and the permafrost rises towards the surface, the tundra turns dark brown all over. Already there have been snowfalls here, showers that melt because the earth is not icy enough to hold them. In another two weeks, permanent snow will arrive in some areas. By the end of October the rivers will be frozen, and by December the sea will be solid, several miles out. At present, though, the temperatures are pleasant, 30 degrees Fahrenheit to about 50 degrees. During this fortnight, the only permanent snow has been a little dust on the mountain tops. In Anchorage this is called 'termination dust', not because it signals the last of summer but because it used to tell the miners in the mountains that it was time to pack up and go down to the town, to avoid being snowed in for the long winter.

I have visited six Eskimo village schools in the Bering Strait area, each time staying overnight in the village: Unalakleet, Gambell on St Lawrence Island, Wales, Shishmaref, White Mountain and Shaktoolik. I have also seen something of the villages of Elim, Koyuk and Brevig, and had a couple of days in the gold shanty town of Nome, which is a real frontier town with no frills.

Each of the Bering Strait villages has its own identity and traditions and the people, both children and elders, have been very forthcoming in sharing the stories of their lives. I felt that in two weeks I learned more than I had in the previous ten years, and I marvelled at the ability of these people to survive well through winters which would reduce our modern twentieth-century living to chaos in a few days. Most of the houses in the villages now have electricity but very few have running water or sewerage. In each village there is now a 'Washetaria' a kind of communal wash/bath-house where people pay to have showers or wash their clothes. But most people still get their water from the river, filling bottles in summer, and in winter, cutting large blocks of ice and hauling them back by sled. In summer the common form of transport is the Honda four-wheeler. In winter it is a motorised snow machine, pulling a wooden snow sled. In villages such as Shishmaref, dogs are still used, ten to twelve huskies pulling a sled.

These days there are no nomadic tribes. All people have their villages but winter and summer they go on 'camps' to follow food sources. Summer brings the salmon to the rivers. People fish with rods and with set nets. The salmon is filleted and hung to dry for winter, on wooden frames outside the houses. Fish dehydrates very well in this dry atmosphere. It is now the end of the long salmon season and most drying racks are full of fish. Upstream, the last of the silver salmon turn red, drop their eggs and then die. On Thursday at White Mountain, I was taken for a ride about ten miles up river, to see some moose. The clear river water had patches of scum and foam caused by decaying salmon. Gulls had flown for miles inland to share the feast with bears.

Food still seems to be abundant in these parts. Seals are shot, their skins scraped by the women with an ulu, a fan-shaped knife, and hung out to dry, their fat rendered down for oil. Moose, caribou and reindeer offer the most common land meats, along with ptarmigan, geese and crane. Storms and big waves wash clams and crabs up on the beach.

Only the Eskimo people may hunt certain species like wolf, walrus, polar bear and whale. Some villages have a tradition of carving walrus tusks and whalebone. At the school in Gambell I was shown the craft room where youngsters are taught carving and skin sewing. There is also an area where they are shown how to butcher seals. Needless to say, the room is built so that it can be washed down afterwards.

In spring, as the ice is breaking, baluga and bow-headed whales migrate up the coast. Whale hunting is still done in the traditional walrus-skin boats. The walrus hides, of elephantine thickness, are split and drawn over wooden frames and then painted a bluish white to look like an iceflow. Aluminium, fibreglass and solid wood boats do not fare so well in the ice. Each boat has about twelve men, including a captain and a striker. The striker's harpoon is still hand-thrown but these days there is an explosive device in the head which kills the whale quickly.

Each village is permitted only so many strikes a year. Some high-school students at Gambel showed me the video they had taken of a whale hunt last year. Bow-headed whales were sighted and instantly everyone on the boat became quiet. Even the paddles didn't make a sound that could be picked up by the recorder. A whale broached in front of the camera. It looked enormous. The students told me it was small, only fifty-seven feet long. Then the boat was on it, so close that the striker threw the harpoon in a downward sweep. I couldn't see what happened next. This was no *Jaws* fake. The camera went wild and everything was a blur of rope, ice, whale, arms and heads, to the sound of jubilant shouts. At the same time, outboard motors kicked into life. These, explained the students, were the other boats coming in to help. The next clear picture was of a cluster of skin boats around the whale and a man standing on top of the creature, pinning its flukes to its sides so that they would not act as sea brakes as they hauled it to shore by the tail. When the whale came ashore, everyone – man, woman, child – came to the beach with their ulus, those fan-shaped knives; to cut it up.

Joy Cowley (left), 'helping' to cut the last bits of frozen meat from a baluga whale. Whale is carefully managed; villages are allowed no more than five strikes a year. Whale meat is essential to the Eskimo diet.

Nothing is wasted. The bone is put into the 'bone yard' where it is later used for carving. The baleen, that dark soft fringe which strains the whale's food, is woven into baskets and jewellery. The meat feeds the entire village for some time. I saw the women cutting off one-inch strips of blubber, rinsing it in seawater and then giving it to their toddlers as a delicacy. (The Eskimo game of 'blanket toss' which is similar to a trampoline, began so that people, tossed high into the air, could see distant whales or other game.)

Also at Gambell, I was treated to a display of Eskimo dancing. Some of the elders came in to assist the high-school students with the singing and drumming while the younger students danced. The drumming is done on birch frames covered with parchment from animal skin or intestines, and tapped with a thin curved stick. The dance stories are elaborate. The children tried to teach me some of the hand movements but even the simplest dances were much too complicated for me.

The sale of carved walrus ivory and whalebone in these villages is legitimate but the people may not sell polar bear skins. The bears have to be shot. They are often drawn to the houses by the quest for food and, at three to four metres high, have no trouble breaking down doors. They are carnivores and dangerous. At Shishmaref I photographed two polar bear skins hanging on a frame to dry: both had been shot near the village. In summer, during salmon time, grizzly bears can also be a problem when they come into camps looking for food. A twelve-year-old girl told me how she had shot four bears in one evening.

Children learn to hunt at a very early age. Hunting here is not an option. It is for survival. Teachers tell me that kids know how to handle guns before they come to school. The principal at White Mountain school has a huge bear skin on his wall – it was shot by a six-year-old. Then, at a parent/teacher reception last Wednesday evening, one of the fathers was saying that his five-year-old son (who was very small) wasn't big enough to handle a gun. 'He nearly shot himself in the foot,' said Dad. 'We'll have to wait until next year.'

The people here have always lived in wooden houses. In pre-European times their roofs were tied-down walrus hides. They have never 'lived' in igloos. The igloo has been the winter camp dwelling, just as the hide tent has been the summer camp abode. The people travel many miles to meet migrating animals or to hunt and fish in traditional places. In winter, one man can make an ice igloo in about half an hour. A sloping entrance is cut in the ice and the wedge-shaped blocks from the cut are stacked round in a snail-shell design, then capped. Traditionally, the people have not had wood fires. Seal oil was burned with a lichen wick, in a pottery dish. This gave light and heat, and also cooked food. An elder assured me that the seal-oil dish would keep the temperature inside an igloo at about 40 degrees Fahrenheit, comfortable for people in thick furs, while outside it could be 30 degrees below freezing. The heat and breath in the igloo would glaze the inside and prevent the wind from coming through any chinks. These days igloos are still made by some people but heated inside with gas burners and bottles.

The children, girls and boys alike, shoot caribou, moose and seals. Seals are shot in the water and then retrieved with a gaff at the end of a rope, thrown like a lasso. There is no question of jumping into the water after them. That is the most dangerous thing which can happen to anyone – falling into the freezing sea. Clad in a neoprene survival suit, a fisherman may last about 10 minutes. Without that, hypothermia and death come within four minutes.

Andy Haveland, the principal at Gambell School, is married to a local woman and lives in the village. About seven years ago, he went with others in several skin boats, on a walrus hunt. It was spring, the ice was breaking and there was a lot of fog. The boats became separated and Andy's boat was lost out at sea. They ran out of fuel trying to get back, and for twenty-one days drifted in the Bering Strait in freezing conditions. They had seal and fish on board to eat but when the last of the ice melted, they became very thirsty. Helicopters came and went above the fog, and then gave up hope. On the twenty-first day a strong wind came up and blew them to the back of St Lawrence Island. Andy said he lost nearly nineteen kilograms in those twenty-one days, not a diet he would recommend. The interesting thing was that none of them suffered from frostbite or hypothermia because they were correctly dressed. The main problem was a bad outbreak of tinea from long-term boot-encased feet.

In these places where temperatures with the wind-chill factor can reach 100 degrees below zero (that is, 130 degrees below freezing point!) the only survival is in layers of animal skins. No part of the body can be exposed. No one can wear metal-rimmed glasses – they cause severe facial burns. Neoprene face masks, such as those worn in the lower latitudes, freeze with the breath and bond onto the skin. But the Eskimo parka, with its double fur lined hood and polar bear ruff which extends far beyond the face, not only prevents freezing but keeps the face comparatively warm.

In this last week people have been very upset by a tragedy out in the sea near Siberia. Demographers doing research from both Russia and Anchorage, together with local people, were in walrus-skin boats which met with some accident. Both boats have been found broken. Two bodies have also been found. No survivors. It seems that the only thing which could have done this would be a wounded whale. Because people in every village seem to know at least one of the eighteen people involved, it has been the main topic of conversation in the villages. A broken boat means death. Life-jackets are useless in this part of the world.

In winter people go ice-fishing in the sea or rivers. A long-handled ice pick chips a hole in the ice and a line with a jigging stick is dropped into the hole for smelt, tomcod, pike, trout, grayling. Ice fishing in the sea is often for big king crab which can be caught simply with a large bait on the end of a line, slowly pulled up.

The sea freezes from the shore out. The first ice breaks, heaps up and refreezes, so that the ultimate solid surface is far from even. A teacher at Wales village told me that she went out walking on the ice when she thought it was solid enough. An Eskimo elder who saw her, told her that this was not smart. Not only was the ice thin in parts, she did not have a walking stick. Apparently you must carry a long pole to test the ice, for in some places, where there is a strong current, the thick white surface is merely snow over thin ice. Also, if you fall in between ice floes, then the pole can be flipped horizontally, each end on a floe, to help you get out.

At Wales I could clearly see the mountains of the Russian mainland on the horizon. The closest US land to Russian territory is Little Diomede Island (Alaska) which is only a few miles from Big Diomede Island (Siberia). I was scheduled to go to Little Diomede by helicopter but there is often fog out there, and that could have marooned me. I was told that Little Diomede is simply a large steep rock, with all the houses built on stilts. The helicopter lands on a wooden platform, also built on stilts. In the winter, when the sea is frozen, the ice is ploughed nat with a road grader, so that a plane can land by the island. 'But how do they know when the ice is thick enough?' I asked. They told me that the grader drives out from the shore. If the ice begins to crack, it makes a rapid retreat. This testing goes on until the grader can go all the way out to the island. The first planes of the winter season to come in to Little Diomede are single-engined light aircraft. As the season progresses and the ice thickens, the twin-engined aircraft come in.

While here, I have flown from village to village in a variety of aircraft, some of which have resembled the old Landrover SWB I used to own – lots of mud, rust and patched bits, and the interior looking and smelling as though it had just taken sacks of coal and fish to market. The pilots seemed to be very careful and capable, though. All flights were in fine weather and, apart from the cold, comfortable enough. The largest aircraft I travelled in was a Beech 99; the smallest were several Stationair 7 and 8. Fellow passengers were usually fishermen, maintenance men flying into villages to fix phones or power, or village people coming out for hospital or dental appointments. The vastness of this land is impressive. You can fly for an hour or more between villages, with no sign of human habitation beneath, just tundra, swamp, sea, snow-creased hills, and more tundra.

But after all this, I still haven't said much about the schools I visited. Again, in each village the school was different and yet all the children shared certain characteristics. They are very open and spontaneous, lively and loving. I was struck by their emotional freedom. They belong to an active culture and find it difficult to sit still. Nor are they particularly attracted to book learning, although, because they have high intelligence, they do well enough in tests. The other thing I noted was their keen sense of observation. They noticed everything about me and were full of questions to cover what they could not observe. I suppose this alertness is part of their hunting background, as are their 'silent' conversations. They have their own sign language. For example, among the Yupik people 'yes' can be verbalised and can also be expressed by raising the eyebrows – useful, I guess, when you are stalking a moose.

Some young people go out to University but generally don't do well. This is not because they are academically below par, but because they lose their identity away from their village. Community is very strong: elders are revered, and older children take care of the young with a sense of responsibility that goes beyond western codes. I was given several receptions at which the teachers had provided snacks. I was intrigued that not all the children ate the cakes and cookies. They would put half a dozen pieces in a paper napkin and take them away, to share with those members of their family who had not been able to come.

Tuberculosis is still active in the villages and children are tested regularly. There was a TB test done in schools this week, and a few tears amongst the littlest ones. The village school caters for all children from pre-school (three-year-olds) to high school. Most of the teachers would be from other American states but there are some Eskimo teachers and many teacher aides from the village who help with the curriculum and also teach cultural subjects.

I had hoped while up here to see the Northern Lights which have now become active. Well, I did and I didn't. The display was a yellowish green flickering in one small part of the sky about 3am one morning. The next day I found that this was limited because most of the sky was covered with cloud. But from now until next spring there will be brilliant displays on clear frosty nights. People tell me it looks like rippling curtains of colour, sometimes yellow or green, sometimes red. It usually occurs in the early hours of the morning.

During mid-winter in the Bering Strait area there is about one hour of 'light' in the middle of the day. The sun lifts half of itself over the horizon to give a dim light and then disappears again a short time later. In mid-summer you can read a book outdoors twenty-four hours of the day. Right now, mid-September, the sun starts coming up very slowly at about 8.30am and goes down again about 10pm with a long twilight to midnight. The curious thing is that, here on the Arctic circle, the sun sets near the place where it rises, doing a slow circle of the sky instead of going across it.

In mid-winter, most villages have a festival of some kind but the State event which captures everyone's imagination is the 1100-mile Iditerod dog-sled race from Anchorage to Nome. This annual event is in commemoration of a dog-sled relay race to Nome to carry medication from Anchorage to treat an epidemic of diphtheria, at the beginning of this century. The original run took about three weeks. The race now is run not as a relay but with one pack of twenty dogs for each entrant, and compulsory rests built in. The race goes through some of these villages – Unalakleet, Shaktoolik and White Mountain. At White Mountain I was given one of the foam plastic bootees with velcro fastening which are used to cover the paws of the racing dogs. The huskies are incredibly strong and can cover a hundred miles a day. One teacher told me about taking her husky dog for a walk in the snow. It spotted a cat and immediately dislocated her shoulder! The injury required weeks of convalescence.

Well, I am writing this in Unalakleet on my last full day in what they call the Alaskan bush. Why bush I don't know, since there is almost no bush as we know it. I think that the term refers to its remoteness. I am sitting with my laptop in a small apartment owned by the Bering Strait School District. The building has several such apartments to house administration staff. Outside the sky is leaden after days of fine weather. There has been some rain with sleet, drops turning magically to fine flower petals which flutter on the wind. It is cold out. I guess that the beautiful autumn is near a close.

Tomorrow I begin the long twenty-four-hour journey home to Terry, spring blossom, green sea and my own home and village.

History *as it* Happens

CK Stead

A Passion for Travel

WHAT WOULD A book launch be like in Zagreb? Kay and I were in Oxford for two terms. There had been a summer holiday in rural France and winter visits to Paris and Stockholm. It was January 1997, an exceptionally – wonderfully – severe English winter, in which the rivers in Oxford had frozen over, and the fountain outside the Radcliffe Infirmary had gradually vanished, first behind the curtain, then under the pile-up, of its own self-created ice. We were close to returning to New Zealand when the message came. A translation into Croatian of my novel *All Visitors Ashore*, which I knew had been in train for some time, was ready for publication, and we were invited to come to Zagreb for a few days at the publisher's expense.

I had no idea what to expect. I knew about the recent Yugoslav war – who could not? – but it seemed such an unhappy and typically human mess I had averted my eyes from its complexities. I was vague about Serb and Croat, Croat and Muslim, about Belgrade and Zagreb and Sarajevo. My thoughts were basic, and superficial. How safe was Air Croatia? How safe were the streets of Zagreb? Would we be holed up in an eastern European hotel, afraid to go out? A friend who had been behind the Iron Curtain both before and since the collapse of communism advised that we should take our own loo paper.

One forgets that, as well as communist austerity for the many, there used to be communist opulence for the few. Some of each survives. I was an official writer and therefore, it soon emerged, to be accorded the status that role used to imply in the communist world before the brutal truths of the marketplace began to be enforced. We were met by my publisher and taken by chauffeur-driven Merc to a hotel, the Esplanade, the lobby of which had enough marble and staircases to suggest, at the very least, a Cecil B de Mille movie-set.

Our suite was no let-down. It was very grand indeed, all maroon and grey stripes, and with its own interior corridor. There were flowers and fruit on the tables, and white bathrobes, his and hers, in the marble bathroom. Our windows looked out past noble pillars and down over a vast snow-covered square with a fountain at the centre, where people, mostly shabbily dressed, waited for blue trams, and equestrian statues from various époques made their historical and political statements in the cold misty light.

We had baulked at the idea of packing a just-in-case roll of loo paper, but there was, in Kay's bag, a precautionary box of Kleenex tissues. She took it out now and put it down on the vast bed where we stared at it for a moment and were both suddenly shaking with laughter. Our welcome had been not so much a pleasant surprise as a pleasant astonishment.

The Esplanade is, I suppose, a hotel of the old Austro-Hungarian empire days, preserved under communism for the nomenclatura, and preserved now by the new Croatian nationalists that the old socialist internationalists have become. Visually, Zagreb is that same mix – empire grandeur, some of it falling into disrepair, along with worker-state drabness.

Two women were partly responsible for our being there – the translator Ljiljana S, and the editor Jadranka P. They had, they said, fallen in love with *All Visitors Ashore;* indeed the book can never have had two more ardent admirers; and they had encouraged the publisher in his plan to launch it in style.

For the next few days we were showered with gifts and entertained lavishly in the best restaurants, which were very good indeed. There was a press conference in a bookshop. There was a meeting with the Minister for the Arts, Bozo Biskupic, shown that evening on national television news. The launch itself was held in a jazz club, BP's, where it seemed all Zagreb's intelligentsia had gathered. There were clever speeches, and a reading from the Croatian version of the novel by a professional actor. There was good jazz, good food, good booze and good jokes. Everyone who came was given a copy of the novel.

I was struck by the scale of the thing, its generosity, and also its oddness. It was as if we had stepped back into a world of privilege – not the old privilege of empire, but the more recent one of communism, which had survived communism's demise. The party and the doctrine were gone, but the habits were not. Only a publisher with official government backing could have spent so much on a book that was distinctly 'literary' and unlikely to make big sales. Yet this was also a publisher who wanted very much to make his way, and prosper, in the new environment of free enterprise and open markets. Of course I was grateful, and enjoyed every minute of it; but I couldn't blind myself to the ironies of history it seemed to encapsulate.

Before we arrived there had been news in Britain of marches in Zagreb in support of the one remaining independent radio station, which had been critical of the Tudjman government and was now threatened with closure. At some point during the evening of the launch I was approached by a young woman saying she represented that station and asking whether I would agree to be interviewed. I said yes and was taken at once to a sort of cupboard under a stairway. There, in almost total darkness, she taped an interview, thanked me, and was gone. It was my visit's only unofficial public moment, and it too felt like a throwback to the days of the Berlin Wall and the Iron Curtain.

In between the official engagements and meals, Ljiljana and Jadranka took Kay and me for walks in Zagreb – up to the old town, to the cathedral, the market, the cable car, the parks and squares – and once, in Jadranka's noisy but dependable Skoda, out of the city to a charming coffee shop in the village of Samobor. There, in the late afternoon as darkness fell, we encountered by chance a local winter folk carnival – people dressed as animals making a variety of hoots and wails, roars and whistles and squeaks, as they paraded along the road.

We were learning all the time about the recent war – the complexity of its politics, the cruelty of its enactment, the pain and fear and anger it had left. Every dinner and every conversation added to one's knowledge and increased one's curiosity and one's sense of how people inherit their history almost as an aspect of personality. On our last night there we met a poet and editor who had remained in exile through all the years of communism, still writing in his own language, and who, on hearing news of Croatia's declaration of independence, had bought a revolver and come home to defend it. Already, of course, being an honest and forthright fellow of high intelligence, he was in conflict with the new government that had welcomed him home as a national hero.

Every writer is a shameful scavenger, and one reaches an age where every new experience presents itself both for what it is and for what might be made of it. By now all these riches were beginning to merge in my mind with thoughts I'd had long before about a novel that might make something of New Zealand's historical links with Croatia, links which no one growing up in the north can be unaware of. I had recollections of farmland still pockmarked by the grave-like holes made by Dalmatian gumdiggers, and of rusty spade-handled gum spears they left behind. And Kay (like Maurice Gee) had spent her childhood among the orchardists and wine-growers of the Henderson Valley west of Auckland. It was a rich furrow, made richer by the recent war.

The following European summer, the novel taking clearer shape in my mind, I returned to Zagreb.

I stayed with Ljiljana, who lived with her aunt in an apartment in central Zagreb. My days were spent there, or walking about the city. Then, each evening, Jadranka, who owned a modern flat in the suburbs, came in her Skoda and took me to a café or restaurant, or for a walk in a park, or to a movie. The plan was that towards the end of that week the three of us would travel to an area on the coast where many New Zealand Dalmatians had come from.

I began to see Ljiljana and Jadranka as representing two separate, even opposed, Croatias which the recent war had pushed into firm unity. Ljiljana's parents had been communist nomenclatura, the father a lawyer and diplomat; and in her student years Ljiljana had been a serious Young Communist. The idealism hadn't lasted; but neither had the world view it implied been entirely discarded. She still tended to see the wealthy nations as having gained their advantages by imperialist exploitation rather than by economic efficiency; and philosophically she was, I'm sure, a rationalist.

Jadranka, on the other hand, was almost certainly from a right-wing Catholic family of the kind that had long ago prospered under the old Austro-Hungarian hegemony, and had suffered least under the Nazi occupation. She represented (if my speculations were right) the Croatia for whom the communist federation of Yugoslavia had been particularly unfortunate.

Neither Ljiljana nor Jadranka was entirely frank on political matters – or I felt they were not – and given the history of their lifetime (they were aged forty and thirty-six) that is not surprising. My feeling, however, was that there was an important underlying difference, like a crack in a wall that is none the less solid. The wall was their common loyalty to Croatia. Like most Croatians, they had resented the dominance of Belgrade in the old Yugoslavia, and the preponderance of Serbs in army and police; and they were indignant at what that army, which had become the army of Serbia, had done to Croatia in its attempts, ultimately unsuccessful, to hold the federation together.

But there had been another, more important, determinant in Ljiljana's life. When she was twelve, living the life of a privileged child of senior communists, both her parents were killed in a car accident. She was returned to the Zagreb apartment where her aunt and uncle occupied one bedroom, her grandmother and grandfather the other. The only remaining space was a small kitchen, a bathroom, and a sort of cupboard room into which, as she grew older, a bed was put for her.

Ljiljana had lived there until she left to be a student in Dubrovnic. Now, after a number of years working for large corporations, during which time both grandparents and the uncle had died, she was back with the surviving aunt, attempting to make a living as a freelance translator and, it seemed, succeeding very well.

On the fifth floor of a grim, grey-faced post-war block in a street of such blocks, the apartment was reached by means of a dark stairway of cracked and stained concrete. There was no lift. The blue trams banged away picturesquely in the street below. A small balcony off the kitchen looked down into an inner courtyard echoing with the voices of many families. To reach the room where Ljiljana slept and worked, you went through the bathroom, where the one tap over the handbasin was cold, and the bath-shower, hidden by a curtain on a wire, was served by an old-style gas calafont. The kitchen was minimal, with space for only a small supply of utensils and equipment. The refrigerator was kept in the hallway, just inside the front door.

I slept in the cupboard room listening to the summer-night voices echoing around the shaft-like courtyard, shouting, singing, arguing, and murmuring in Croatian. I relished the flavour of it, the richness, the sense that this was like a short ride back into central Europe's recent past. I had loved the opulence of the Esplanade hotel, but this was better!

Rebecca West records her impression of Zagreb as a kind of gymnasium of the intellect, and Ljiljana was that formidable person, a central-European intellectual, her room full of books and heavy with smoke. At all hours of the day we smoked (I reverted briefly to the habit) and talked books, politics, movies, music – and then books again. Around two each afternoon the aunt, whose name was Kristina and who spoke no English, called us to the table, barely big enough for three, in the tiny kitchen where she had cooked lunch. There was a particular food style which I suppose must be typical of the region, and distinct from the Dalmatian style I would later experience. I remember especially delicious stews, with stuffed peppers and marrows, rich in garlic, and a thick tasty soup-like juice.

Kristina seemed to enjoy her role as Ljiljana's mother-figure, and as hostess to the 'famous visiting writer', about whom she held daily news conferences for inquisitive neighbours on the apartment stairs.

Later in the day came the change of gear which my evenings with Jadranka represented. Jadranka, Ljiljana assured me, was 'the real intellectual'; but since her English was imperfect and my Croatian non-existent, communication at that level was impossible. Jadranka laughed a lot, and used the English language recklessly, like a drunk at the wheel of a powerful car. Once, in a restaurant, she recommended that I have the lamb because I came from New Zealand and was 'used to eating ships'. Another time, attempting to explain the meaning of a restaurant's name, she told me that the first word meant forest, and the second meant ... There was a pause while she tried to remember the word in English that would follow forest. 'Vell,' she said. 'It means ...' And then with a rush, 'It means a middle-aged house for knits.'

It took some time to work out that she meant a house for knights of the Middle Ages, and the word she was seeking was court. The restaurant's name in English was Forest Court.

In a cinema, when the movie suddenly stopped and the theatre went dark, she got up and made her way to the back. A minute later she shouted something from the projection room, and the audience broke into laughter. When the movie started up again and she returned to her seat, I asked her the reason for the laughter. It was because she had called out to let everyone know what she'd found there – the reel finished and needing to be changed, and the projectionist sound asleep.

The day came for our trip to the coast to begin and the three of us set off in the roaring, shuddering Skoda, smoking, laughing, arguing, listening to tapes of a Croatian ballad singer whose name on the copy I have appears to be Reno Abore, and whose songs, atmospheric in themselves, still conjure for me the strangeness and richness of that journey. I had seen many images of the war that had taken place in the countryside. There was a time when they had been a daily item on television. So the shock I felt at my first sights of the destruction was itself a shock. Television is not, it seems, reality; and by that I don't mean that it misrepresents, only that, for whatever reason, the impact of the image and of the real are totally different, chalk and cheese.

I think we can't have been more than fifty kilometres south of Zagreb when we encountered the first of the war zones – burned-out houses, collapsed roofs, pockmarked walls, shell-holes, abandoned crops, tiny villages entirely emptied of their inhabitants. Now and then there was a single family living in the ruins of what had been their home. In one place a very small child standing in the doorway of a burned-out house was the only living creature I saw in a wrecked village.

These shocks were to continue at intervals all the way to the coast. I wanted to stop and take photographs, but I was conscious that this might seem insensitive, and I raised the question tentatively. Jadranka's response was not encouraging. Sometimes she drove on as if she hadn't heard. Other times she suggested there could be an armed madman about in the ruins who might take a shot at me; or that there might still be mines laid along the road's edge.

Perhaps she was genuinely afraid for me, or wisely cautious. What I couldn't then determine was whether or not a political element came into it. Certainly whenever I asked whether a destroyed village was Croat or Serb she answered that it was Croat – another example of Serbian barbarism. I knew that although this must often be true, it couldn't always be so. Croats had also engaged in 'ethnic cleansing', especially in the Serb-dominated Krajina region around the city of Knin. Ljiljana said nothing during these exchanges (tentative on my part, crisp on Jadranka's); but later, alone, she confirmed my supposition. Not every ruin we passed was the work of Serbs.

Quite early in this passage through the war zones there was a pause, a change of circumstance and mood. About 120 kilometres south of Zagreb, as the road took us through a forest, Jadranka pulled into a car park outside what looked like a hunting lodge. We had coffee there;

but this was in fact an entrance to the national park of Pritvicka Jezera, a region of woods and interconnected lakes, rivers and waterfalls, so beautiful it seemed unreal, or super-real. We walked there for more than two hours but could, it seemed, have gone on all day without exhausting it. Our route took us down into deep gullies, around small deep lakes, along the edge of streams, the water everywhere an astonishing pale blue, the woods crowding overhead an intense green, while out of holes in rock faces waterfalls plunged, sometimes five or six into a single deep clear pool, where fish hung suspended like balloons or kites in an upside-down sky. A ferry took us across a small lake, after which we decided it was time to climb back to our starting point and continue our journey.

In the war zone.

So it was the lovely countryside again, and at intervals the burned-out villages. Once Jadranka stopped to hunt for something in a handbag and I got out, risking the wildflowers that might be mined at the road's edge, and the concealed madmen among the ruins, to get my pictures. Jadranka wasn't pleased. 'Vas that *destroyed* enough for you?' she asked as I returned.

The landscape was changing now as we climbed a mountain range, leaving behind the lush pastures, the crops and woodlands of the plain. These slopes were littered with loose white stones, the trees low to the ground and widely separated. We stopped for coffee at a bucolic restaurant, enjoying, through gaps in the walls that appeared to have been blasted by artillery shells, wide views of the passes below.

As we came down the other side of the range the familiar Mediterranean-Adriatic colours and patterns began to appear – a landscape of vines and olives, pines and cypresses, orange-red roofs and yellow-orange walls, with the intense pale-into-dark blues of the Adriatic a recurring background. Now we were in Dalmatia, still with evidence from time to time of the recent war, but the coast, or this part of it, seeming to have returned pretty much to what it had been before the fighting began.

Zaton, where the mother and aunt of one of Jadranka's friends had said they would look after us, is a small fishing village not far from the town of Sibenik, at the end of an estuary into which three rivers flow. As you come in from the coast road you look down the estuary and see, perhaps three or four kilometres away, the white church at the centre of the village, and the yellows and oranges of the buildings clustered around it. As you get nearer you see its cafés, a few shops, a restaurant perched over the water, and many small brightly painted fishing boats. On the hills behind the houses of the village are small holdings, vineyards, vegetable gardens, olive groves.

Since I no longer remember their names I will have to call the two elderly sisters who, separately, welcomed us to Zaton, Aunt A and Aunt B. They were of peasant stock, widows, partisans (along with their husbands) during World War II, communists who had prospered under Tito's Yugoslavia but now, it seemed, loyal Croatian nationalists. Aunt A told me (through Ljiljana's translation) that when she first married she moved into a modest house occupied by twenty-four members of an extended family. She and two other young wives of three brothers took turns to cook for the whole household. The meal was prepared in a cauldron, and the family sat around it and ate from it. Every summer as many as twenty, or even thirty, children from the village, mostly babies and infants, would die of diseases that seemed to arrive with the hot weather.

Jadranka wanted to know how anyone in those circumstances had found a way to get pregnant. Ah, the old lady said, her expression for a moment happy at the retrospect, they had gone out into the fields and the woods for that. Later, when we visited Aunt B, she showed us a very small room, reached by a ladder through a trapdoor from the floor below, in which, in those pre-war days, a family of two adults and four children had lived.

Now Aunt A had her own pleasant house in Zaton. In her late seventies, she was still a big strong healthy woman who each day climbed the hill behind the house to tend her goats and hens, her vines and vegetables. Aunt B, who had been a schoolteacher, owned several rooms opening off an enclosed lane in the village, and also an apartment in Sibenik, her principal dwelling place.

Aunt A greeted us with the traditional welcome of the region – a dish of almonds, and small glasses of her own plum brandy, colourless and with a kick like a mule. Later, when we were washed and rested, there was a meal she had prepared for us – three kinds of fish, straight from the boats, each cooked in a different way, with courgettes and kale rich in garlic, and her own red wine taken (as was the habit of the region) with water. That, however, was not to be the end of eating. There was, Jadranka explained, a certain rivalry between the two widowed sisters, and Aunt B had also cooked us a meal which politeness demanded we should not refuse.

The day had been hot and humid and while we prepared to move on, the air seemed to press down until rain began to fall – warm, heavy, drumming on the vine leaves outside the open windows, with sudden forks of lightning, very near, and thunder like the snapping of huge branches. Under umbrellas Ljiljana, Jadranka and I made our way down into the village, sloshing through the warm flooded streets to Aunt B's and another heroic engagement with food. My recollection is that it was chicken, with a cucumber and tomato salad, very good but of course too good, and too much; and because I was male and (it was agreed) not quite as fat as a man of my age ought to be, the onus of doing justice to it fell on me.

That night, back at Aunt A's, I slept well despite waking at intervals to the most extraordinary conjunction of summer-night noises – a snoring giant in a nearby house, a chiming clock loud enough to suggest that it belonged to the giant, roosters crowing at the moon, the clatter of goat-hooves, and loudest of all (there is surely no other sound in nature quite like it) Aunt A's donkey practising his scales.

Next day Ljiljana, Jadranka and I took a ferry from Sibenik, two hours' brisk chug to the island of Prvic, from which, I was told, so many had gone to New Zealand that it had sometimes been referred to locally as Zealandia. There was a small village, not exactly flourishing but still inhabited. But in our walk around the foreshore, and later, after swimming off a stone jetty, when we made our way 'inland' and got lost among vineyards and olive groves mostly abandoned to weeds and blackberry, we encountered only three or four people.

The following day we visited Primosten, a perfectly circular 'almost-island' (as Tennyson describes Sirmione) joined to the mainland by a neck of land only wide enough for a single road, the join itself possibly man-made. The very small town which completely fills the circle seems, much of it, to have been preserved from medieval times. From the church and graveyard on the highest point, one looks out in all directions over the bland blue Adriatic, with islands floating near and far, a sort of Hauraki Gulf, perhaps even more beautiful, dreamier, but without the clarity and sharp definition.

Back on the mainland we swam and lay in the sun among smooth white stones, or in the shade of pines. It was there that Ljiljana and I had a protracted argument about the behaviour of a male character in one of my novels, until Jadranka, who could not enter into the fast cut-and-thrust of it, grew impatient with both of us, and perhaps also with the persistence of the English language which my presence imposed.

After our day in the sun we decided to eat at a restaurant. We sat in a small courtyard, open to the sky and enclosed by an ancient wall of white stone out of which a single fig tree grew, hanging leaves and fruit over our table. Jadranka and I had a seafood risotto and salad, with wine and followed by ice-cream, while Ljiljana, who always lost her appetite in public places, sat smoking. When we came out it was almost dark and a full moon was rising.

It had been very jolly in the restaurant until Jadranka had noticed her watch was missing. She valued it especially because it had been given by her sister, and I wanted us to return to the beach and look for it, but she refused, insisting the loss was a 'sign', a reminder to her, a punishment for happiness. 'I vas not meant to be happy,' she assured me. On the drive back to Zaton the two women quarreled, briefly but fiercely, in darkest Croatian, which seems equipped with an armoury of extra consonants for such occasions.

At Aunt A's house Jadranka, who had announced an intention to greet the full moon with inebriation, downed two good glasses of the welcoming plum brandy and suggested we walk into the village. We set off, brayed away by the donkey. On the narrow road below the village graveyard Jadranka stopped to pray at a wayside shrine to the Virgin. Ljiljana and I looked past one another, down at the ground and up at the night sky, while Jadranka knelt there on the hard stones, her lovely dark head bowed to the pale plaster Madonna, her small hands clasped tight. The sceptic in me couldn't believe it was so much a prayer as a piece of theatre, of melodrama. And whatever it was, in that region where the murderous divisions call themselves ethnic but are really religious, I would have been true to form if I'd felt at the very least impatient. But within myself it seemed I'd entered a world of comedy. Maybe, unlike Jadranka, I 'vas meant to be happy' – sometimes, anyway.

Jadranka and C K Stead in Zagreb the previous winter.

Zaton under the big moon was unbelievably beautiful, the fishing boats set in glass, the tables outside the two cafés full of fine handsome people and, by a stroke of luck, a klapa group – six male singers in white shirts, dark trousers and embroidered waistcoats – entertaining the village with traditional Croatian songs, sometimes accompanying themselves on mandolins, guitars, zithers, sometimes unaccompanied, always in three or four-part harmony. The music, passionate, primitive, full of pain and full of hope, was like an indicator of Dalmatia's location – Greek-Italian, or Italian-Greek, between the two, with something of each and with something that was neither. Love songs, songs about war, songs about immigration – Ljiljana translated for me. I wrote out the words of one, thinking of the Dalmatians who had come to New Zealand from this beautiful region and climate, and whom too easily we expected to be simply happy, grateful for their good fortune: 'In vain my mother told me/ The sea never returns what you give it/ Not the people and not the ships./ In vain she told me/ In vain she cried/ The sea was stronger/ And my ship sails tonight.'

Jadranka's sober self fought the alcohol valiantly, and we sat on and on, enjoying the music and the scene, until at last and suddenly it was apparent that the sober self had lost. Returning home we had to restrain her from diving into the harbour. In the middle of the road, close to the statue of the Virgin which by now she had forgotten, she lay down on her back, laughing helplessly and blowing smoke rings at the moon.

A few days later, driving back to Zagreb, Jadranka, as if she had inwardly relented, or ceased to be defensive, or decided to be trusting, took the route she had avoided on the way down – through the Krajina, and even into Knin, where we stopped for coffee. Where were all the people? It was a question I didn't need to ask. There were a few about; but it was as if we had gone into Hamilton, or Dunedin (I mean a town of that size) on a Sunday morning.

'Yes,' Jadranka admitted. 'The Serbs are gone.'

I wanted to know how they had left.

'On foot', she said. They had been given the chance to go, and they had gone.

I tried to imagine the scene – the victorious Croatian army, fine young men like the Klapa singers, but grim, silent, armed, threatening, watching as people who had lived there all their lives filed out on foot, knowing they were leaving their homes and their region for ever.

That was bad enough. It was best not to dwell at all on the worse things that had been done in this region in the name of independent Croatia – the work of the 'Autumn Rains' unit, for example, whose luckiest Serbian victims were the ones killed with a single bullet to the forehead.

To think like that, putting Croatia in the wrong, was to forget all the wrongs which had brought that action about – all of Serbia's murderous ethnic cleansing, practised against Croat and Muslim alike. But then, did one fact excuse another? And this, as it happened, was the fact that confronted me: a once flourishing town emptied of the larger part of its population only because they were Serbs.

All at once I understood more clearly why Jadranka had not wanted me to see certain things, nor to ask certain questions. Laying blame is so easy, especially at a distance. But our history is not of our own making or choosing, and whatever it happens to be we have to live with it and make the best of it.

Trying to be 'philosophical', I said something to the effect that war was, perhaps, only life intensified.

'Intensified?' They didn't understand.

'Sped up,' I suggested. 'The bad things happen faster.' I was struggling. 'Sooner.'

'Oh my god,' Ljiljana said, smiling and patting my hand indulgently. 'You're beginning to sound like one of us.'

Of Bonaparte *and* Blue Suede Shoes

_____

Sarah Quigley

OUR EYES MEET across a crowded ferry. He looks interested. I look as uninterested as a month in Paris has taught me how. It doesn't work. He keeps staring over his moustache, I lose my French cool and resort to Kiwi caginess.

'That guy keeps staring at me,' I mutter.

'Colour this in, would you?' says Dave. He is engrossed in making a sign out of a flattened *frites* carton. The sign says 'Calvi' and he hopes it will get us somewhere near there in the next two hours, or twenty.

I colour in Calvi with a red mini-marker, inhaling religiously. All I smell is garlic. I look up to see the middle-aged moustache standing beside me. I'm glad I'm travelling with a boy. I look like a boy in my hitching gear anyway, so I can't see why he's even bothering.

'Allez-vous,' I mutter. 'Au revoir, arsehole.'

'Calvi?' he says in an Italian accent. 'I am going there and I will take you there in my car, you and your frrriend.'

He isn't our enemy, he's our frrriend. He's a good guy. I love handle-bar moustaches and the smell of partially digested garlic.

It's all very well being fly-by-the-seat-of-your-pants travellers, but this time it means arriving in Corsica at 3am. We go on deck and strain sleep-deprived eyes towards Bastia, fifteenth-century stronghold of the Genoese, but we don't see anything except twentieth-century docks. Five minutes from the Port Nouveau, we've read, are flamboyant Baroque churches and mysterious vaulted passageways but our driver seems to be in a hurry. We fly along the avenue du Maréchal Sébastiani and exit Bastia in a blur of lights.

Soon it's dark. Extremely dark. We'd expected to drive north around Cap Corse but our driver takes to the mountains. He knows a shortcut which means we can be with our friends before breakfast. The shortcut has no lights, and no claim to the title of road. We career around hairpin bends and I have serious doubts that we'll live to see another croissant.

Dave, who has strong views on hitchhiker's etiquette, struggles with polite conversation. 'Bit of a language barrier,' he whispers over his shoulder.

It seems more like an insurmountable wall than a barrier to me. After a very long time, Dave manages to ascertain that we are in the car with Giovanni, who has been to the mainland to pick up a prescription for his wife.

'Drugs,' Giovanni says with relish.

I remind myself he is a good guy.

I'm half-asleep when suddenly the car stops. Giovanni leaps out and begins rummaging through the back of the car. Minutes pass, his rummaging becomes more and more violent, and he begins muttering maniacally under his breath. I don't know much Italian but swear words are obvious in any language. I think: so much for the good guy. I think: axes, guns.

'What the fuck's he looking for?' Dave hisses.

There's no sound except for Giovanni's anger. I'm just about to start screaming when Giovanni re-enters the car with a small rectangular object in his hand.

'Cyndi Lauper!' he says.

'Huh?' Dave says.

'Cyndi will keep me awake,' Giovanni explains.

We hurl on to the strains of 'All Through the Night'. My life stretches ahead of me again like the road and I open the window. Far below and to the right, I can see the glimmer of the sea.

We get the good guy to let us out at a bend in the middle of nowhere which Dave assures me is the drive to the villa, only he can't find it so we scramble through scrub and over mud-banks. The others have given up on us and locked the door so we have to climb in through the shutters, dragging our packs behind us.

Next day we can see our footprints weaving a line up the hill, about two metres away from the driveway. The others kindly point out a huge key in a huge white envelope, left on the doorstep for us the night before.

L'Ile Rousse is our closest town and we go there every day to buy supplies, to sit, watch, walk. Crammed with flower boxes, glossy shops and palm trees, it seems more like the French Riviera than a part of rugged Corsica. The heart of the town is place Paoli, a shady square lined with cafés, overlooking the sea. We quickly adopt Chez Paco as our place, sit under awnings and eat huge cheap platefuls of fresh calamari.

In the middle of the square is a fountain, on top of the fountain is a bust of Pascal Paoli. 'Grandfather of the Nation', founder of L'Ile Rousse, and a Corsican hero. He gained fourteen years of independence for the island but was ousted in 1769, and France has ruled ever since.

It's August, height of the tourist season, and the French very obviously rule right now. For the past two months they have flocked to the island, by plane from Nice and Paris, by ferry from Marseilles and Toulon. They're tolerated for their francs. The rest of the year Corsicans fill the bars, which are open twenty-four hours.

'You never see any money change hands then,' says Dave. He raises his eyebrows.

Sunset at L'Ile Rousse. The island which gives the town its name isn't really an island because you can walk to it. Over a neck of land onto a floating head of red rock. The volcanic colours remind me of New Zealand: I crunch over red gravel and for a minute I'm back on a Remuera footpath. Then I turn and see the town glowing in reflected red light, see the huge pink seafront hotel, rugged bare hills, tiny villages, olive trees.

It's Corsica all right – though the light, clarity, space, still speak to me of home.

The days settle into a routine alien to British body clocks. Many of our afternoons are spent sleeping, under trees or in the villa. The beaches empty out under the hot breath of the sun. A lot of our money is spent on suncream and bottled water. A lot of our time is spent eating and drinking.

There are six of us. Every day we buy twelve baguettes and every

Love, peace, on a Corsican beach.

day they all disappear. Bread is served on the side with everything: dipped in bowls of coffee or olive oil, eaten with fresh tomatoes (which taste nothing like the genetically engineered ones sold in London supermarkets). There's a strange attitude to bread here, I realise – it's baked, bought, and consumed with something approaching religious devotion, yet it's stuck under armpits or in saddlebags, thrown on the table instead of on a plate, is grasped, gripped, ripped. At first I find it hard to join in with the abuse of the baguette, but by the end of a month I'm gripping and ripping with the best of them.

'Where's the cottage cheese?' Carol asks plaintively.

She's from England and so, she discovers, is cottage cheese. She asks for it in English, French, and Italian, but no one here has heard of

A Passion for Travel

it. Our French friend Chantal steers her towards the deli counter at the Super U. 'Try this,' she says. She spears a piece of Fromage Corse and holds it out enticingly. It is made in the sheep-rearing central regions. It is very hard. It is very pungent. It smells like very, very old Stilton.

Carol recoils in horror. She resigns herself to the *brocciu* (a harmless-looking fromage frais), and to putting on weight for the rest of the holiday.

Like France, Corsica is a vegetarian's nightmare and a gourmet's paradise. Here they eat anything which runs, flies, swims, or just sits around on rocks. Most restaurants offers stew and it could be anything – kid, hare, wild pig, partridge.

'Or French politician,' says Dave darkly.

Stifatu is hard to buy for love or money. It's a mixture of rolled meats which apparently locals devour daily but restaurants rarely serve. Finally, triumphantly, we stumble upon it in a Calvi restaurant called La Santa-Maria.

'Santa Maria!' says Steve. 'Stifatu at last.'

Like most long-pursued goals, it's a letdown. It's robbed of its authentic local flavour because we're surrounded by British tour groups talking nostalgically of Torquay. We're forced to drown our disappointment with copious amounts of muscat.

Lunch in Porto, a seaside town renowned for its seafood. I see sardines on a menu and snigger, remembering picnics when I was six and tins full of tiny processed stinkers. I order crêpes and think they're great until I see the guy next to me hoeing into a succulent whole fish, stuffed with some divine mixture involving roasted chestnuts.

'Ees sardine,' the olive-skinned waiter assures me.

Dave sniggers.

In our second Corsican week, we decide to visit Napoleon. The train to Ajaccio is like a Tonka toy, yellow, chunky – and cheap.

Pastel-shaded Ajaccio is a serious town. It has a port, it has an airport. It's way bigger than Bastia and way better than anywhere. It has the chic-est cafés, the glossiest shops, the mildest climate, and the greatest number of tourists. It's a bit like Auckland.

'Napoleone' is the town's claim to fame but we soon find that in 1793, chased by Paoli's troops, he fled to France, Gallicised his name, and never returned to Corsica. The locals prefer not to speak of this. Their town is one big monument to the famous emperor so we can traverse his life in an afternoon. We visit the Maison Bonaparte where he frolicked as a baby, we dip our hands in the cathedral font where he was baptised, and we view a replica of his deathmask in the Salon Napoléonien. Actually, I view a postcard of the replica of the deathmask because I am not allowed through the grim doors of the Hôtel de Ville – the skirt I am wearing is too short. This means I also miss out on several important fragments (of his coffin, of his dressing case, of the second button on his second-best coat).

To fill in time I stride. I stride down a cours Napoléon, a quai Napoléon, an avenue Napoléon, and a rue Bonaparte. I begin to wonder if Edward Lear was right when he said that, on a wet day, it would be hard to find a place as dull as Ajaccio. But it is fine, and to my left the sea is as blue as it always is in Corsica, and up in front of me is the ancient Citadelle. Built in the 1490s, it stands high above a yellow beach, looks across the bay to high blue mountains. An old man is sitting on a wall drinking pastis. I ask him in my Anglo-French what he thinks of Napoleon.

'French bastard,' he spits. 'He never was a Corsican.' He gives me a capful of pastis which makes my tongue feel like sandpaper.

I meet up with the others in the Jardins du Casone under a huge bronze statue of the French bastard riding a horse. 'What do we do now?' Dave asks. Looking at the emperor's Roman dress reminds me: the name Ajaccio comes from the Roman word meaning Place of Rest. So we make like the old shepherds who used to stooge down from the mountains to refuel. We find the rue Fesch and stock up with charcuterie sandwiches and Cap Corse wine (fortified, flavoured with herbs, easier on the stomach than pastis). We spend the evening in Le Menestrel with some local musicians who play the mandolin, and then we take in a trashy disco. Even Lear would have enjoyed himself.

Corsican females are recently emancipated. Every big town we visit, we see the new breed of career women. They wear beautiful suits and cover their beautiful skin with Lancôme imported from the mainland. 'Their whole salaries are spent on looking good,' says Chantal-the-French, approvingly.

The Corsican men remain obstinately, charmingly, chauvinist. On the bus to Corte, every male springs up to offer me his seat. Steve has a strapped-up ankle after too much Cap Corse and too many steps. He is glanced at dismissively and made to stand for fifty kilometres.

Corte is the centre of the island, and the centre of the nationalist movement. Corsica's first National Constitution was drawn up there in 1731 and, in 1755, the ubiquitous Paoli made it the capital of his brief republic. 'Strange to have a capital so far away from a port,' says Dave in that wise, deeply critical, male way.

It's a tiny town with only one main street. But its historical significance is huge, and it seems to have a more contemporary relevance than Ajaccio, the present capital which claims only past glories. Corte is the site of the first Corsican printing press and also the first university, founded by Paoli in the 1760s.

'And then closed by the French until 1981,' says Dave critically.

'After the rise of nationalism in the 1970s,' reads Steve wisely.

Corte, Corsica's version of Dunedin. The students give it a heartbeat and there's enough beauty and culture to make for happy tourists. Cobbled streets wind up to the *ville haute* and the Gothic-looking citadel, which houses anachronistic contemporary art exhibitions. The Palais National, the only remaining Genoese building, stands at the gates of the citadel. It used to be the seat of government, then became the university where education was provided free by Franciscan monks. Now it incorporates modern buildings and is an institute for the study of Corsican history and culture.

Old and new. Tradition and freedom. Ancient dust, seductive glitter. This town in the middle of mountains and gorges seems to encapsulate the best of Corsica.

I look pensively in the window of a deeply expensive shoeshop.

'Don't you wish you could participate in a revolution?' says Carol.

'Or are you wishing for a pair of deeply expensive shoes,' says Steve.

Actually, both of them are right and since we happen to be in a country where women are celebrating their emancipation by looking good, I blow a week's hitching money on some blue suede slingbacks.

The tiny woman in black sits in front of her door, rocking, sucking on her gums. She is the old breed of Corsican female, treated not badly but simply as an inferior species. Yet she has a dignity of her own. We feel as if we're intruding but she invites us into her tiny dark kitchen for *fougazi* – big flat biscuits with the kick of anis – and lemon cordial. Then she leads us to the village shop so we can buy stamps. She speaks to the shopkeeper in Corsican, which sounds like a mixture of French, Italian, and Welsh.

The streets are hardly wide enough to ride a bike through, and you wouldn't want to anyway because they turn into frequent flights of steps and do 180-degree turns. We wander slowly, meet children and dogs and donkeys. Most of the long hot afternoon is spent in the tiny village square where we drink beer and play chess. We look down on grey crags and grey shingled roofs. The church bells tell us how slowly time is passing.

We want to stay, we linger. It's evening when we walk back down from high Belguedere to the coast. The long valley ends in a silver triangle of sea. The leaves of the olive trees imitate the silver glint. We want to sleep out under the fierce bright foreign stars, but 'camping sauvage' is forbidden because of fire risk.

'Ironic,' says Dave, looking around us. The landscape has changed to a blackened stunted moonscape. The earth is charred. Not campers' fire but nationalist arson. Once we're back on the main road we see bullet holes in the road signs, 'FLNC' spray-painted on the walls of a new house. This is the work of the Liberation Front, who are violently protesting against economic neglect and want the French central government to leave. Crazy, proud, loyal people, who would rather desecrate their land than have it used by foreigners.

At the next junction is a new mansion, never lived in, gutted like a fish. Built for French holiday-makers by local tradesmen (who are paid out before damage is incurred), it has been bombed by separatists. Violence hangs in the air like church-bells.

Dave ties his bandanna around his head to soak up the sweat and ends up looking like the national emblem. I look back up the valley where black hillsides meet serene grey rock and think about Waitangi and the Moutua Gardens and the price of independence.

Also on our visiting list of the famous and infamous are Christopher Columbus and Lord Nelson. Both can be found in Calvi – just twenty kilometres along the coast from L'Ile Rousse, so they're practically in our neighbourhood. We catch a ride south in an immaculate jeep driven by an immaculate legionnaire, who fills us in on the military history of Calvi.

'You know Nelson?' he says.

'Oui oui,' we agree.

'The leetle English sheet?' he says.

Dave looks mutinous, Chantal laughs, I remain smugly neutral in my Pacific Rim guise.

'He lost his eye in Calvi,' says the legionnaire with enormous satisfaction.

We leave him at a bar in the old quarter with his cronies from the French Foreign Legion. During non-drinking hours, they tell us, they hang out in their garrison in the citadel. 'Live in Corsica have citadel,' I say.

We go there first, walking up eighty metres of granite promontory. Here the Genoese transformed fishing shacks into bastions and built a huge cathedral, L'Eglise St-Jean Baptiste, on the highest point. Inside (I am wearing a long skirt today and can go in unchallenged) is a beautiful ebony icon of Christ. Once brandished at marauding Turks, it is still credited with saving the day.

Next door stands the house where *Christophe Colomb* got his first glimpse of what was to be a wide, wide world. There is a statue of him outside which looks startlingly modern. 'Dude!' says Steve admiringly.

'Erected on 20 March 1992,' intones a tour guide beside us.

'Why then?' asks Chantal, wanting information without paying for it.

'The 500th anniversary of his discovery of America,' imparts the tour guide.

'Shouldn't "discovery" be in inverted commas?' I say reprovingly. I'm thinking international issues here: the moa hunters, the Maori, the marching colonialists.

The tour guide looks even more reproving than me. Anniversaries are big business in Corsica and shouldn't be taken lightly. She ignores me. 'His *alleged* birthday in October is now a public holiday,' she says to her group.

Meekly, I realise that phrases such as 'according to local tradition' must not be argued with.

We walk along the ramparts which encircle the castle. The view is staggering. Dave swears that he can see the villa. We can all see the bay. And the mountains, and the long curve of the Golfe de Calvi. The beach tempts us down into the *ville basse* again, where we become trapped in souvenir stalls and ice-cream stands.

The faded glamour of it all reminds me of the south coast of

England. Where there used to be arms smugglers and 1950s European glitterati, now there are saggy French grandpères and Italian bambini guzzling Coke. What the hell – we join them.

'I wanna do the GR20,' says Chantal. She is eating her fourth croissant of the morning, even though it isn't 9am yet. How do French women stay so goddam thin?

We tell her that the hike runs the length of Corsica. She shrugs in a Gallic way. We tell her that it's also known as Li Monti ('between the mountains') and it includes cables, ladders, and sheer rock faces. She's undaunted. When we tell her that she has to walk 160 kilometres and it sometimes snows, even in July, she says ça va.

Luckily, just as she's reaching for her latté, Dave mentions that the huts are basic as hell and all food supplies have to be carried in. Chantal thinks of powdered milk, and decides that a day trip to the Gorge de la Restonica will probably satisfy her.

We hitch as far as Corte, then stand hopefully with our thumbs out on the D936, the road running south-west up the valley. Actually, it looks as though getting a ride won't be the problem – getting *anywhere* once we're in a car will be the tricky part. Minibuses and Fiats are banked solid. So we hire motor scooters and career along the edge of the traffic jam.

'Look right!' Steve shouts.

'Don't look right!' Dave shouts.

There's a hundred-metre drop into the valley below, with only a few chestnut trees to break the fall into the glacial river. 'You're all wusses,' I shout. 'Where I come from, our state highways are like this.'

The carpark at the bottom of the climb is as packed as the road. The mountain is called Rotondo, and most of the tourists look as if it's been named after them. They sit under raffia umbrellas like immovable boulders, and throw burgers and frites down their throats in the manner of Homer Simpson. 'Look like they couldn't climb a flight of steps,' mutters Dave scornfully.

When a hot-dog vendor tells him how long it takes to get to the top, he pales. But he's only concerned for the rest of us who probably couldn't manage a nine-hour round climb. He decides we'll leave the summit for another day.

The feeling of height after an hour and a half is not only enough, it's amazing. All around us are granite peaks splashed with tiny blue lakes. The forest falls away far below us, dark green sliced with grey banks and white water. Our gaze follows the finger of the valley to the west coast and the glint of the Mediterranean. We stand and look into the indigo depths of Lac de Mélo. You could throw a stone from side to side, but drop one in and it wouldn't touch bottom. The sun is warm, the wind icy. Corsica, country of extremes.

As we jump and scramble back down, there's no one else in sight. Tough maritime pines cling in the corner of rocks, the jagged head of Rotondo rears like a dinosaur behind us. Wilderness. Isolation. Beauty. We round a corner and nearly take out a giant Coke can. A red-and-white vendor sits behind his portable stall chewing gum. We skid to a stop. 'Merde!' he says, and tries to relieve us of our change.

Commercialism. Consumeritis. Multi-national corporations. Corsica, country of contradictions.

They don't know anything about New Zealand. All through France, I've been fielding nuclear comments. It's restful being here – Nouvelle Zélande might as well be as Narnia or Never-Never Land. Chantal gets attitude, the Brits get patronised, I get smiles.

Although I'm from a galaxy far, far away, there's a feeling of familiarity about Corsica which I haven't had anywhere else in Europe. Something to do with the independence of the people and the uneasy relationship with their long-term, smothering 'motherland'. Something to do with the diverse landscape, where white beaches and sheer cliffs and pine forests are close neighbours. Something to do with being able to walk along a one-lane dirt road and seeing a hawk against the dazzle of an unpolluted sun.

Early morning. I get out of my bunk for the last time, put my running shoes on, prepare to race the sun. The hill behind our villa waits for me, the paper sky waits for colour. In a month of mornings, I still haven't made it to the top. The logging road is churned up with the footsteps of trucks. It's hard going and there's a corner where my lungs usually say stop.

Today I keep running. I can see the rim of the hill burning, and the day is taking its last deep breaths of cool air. My eyes hurt, my legs hurt, my whole body complains. I don't listen. I reach the summit, double up, straighten up.

The sea and the sky are fresh and smooth like clean sheets. Where they fold into each other, on the horizon, is deepest blue. The red island floats in a crumpled bay, and the eyes of its buildings are gold. The sun bursts over the mountain ridge and sets a light to the maquis. Its scent rises around me: thyme, marjoram, basil, fennel, rosemary.

'*I used to close my eyes,*' says a nostalgic voice in my head.

'Huh?' I say.

It's Napoleon.

'*And know I was in Corsica because of its scent,*' says poor, exiled Napoleon.

I follow his example, shut my eyes, breathe in. He's right, it's unmistakably Corse. He's right but I'm different, because I know I'll come back.

Neighbourhood Wars *in* Belvoye

Lloyd Jones

A Passion for Travel

AS A YOUNG girl my wife once spent a weekend with an Orthodox Jewish family in Crown Heights, Brooklyn, New York. Years later, she would recall how impressed she was by the rituals they attached to things which the rest of us hardly ever think about. When they opened the fridge they didn't just open the fridge, they said a prayer of thanks for the treasure chest humming in the corner of the kitchen. When they woke up each morning it was not with a frown for the average weather piled up in the window but with a smile, and then they muttered another prayer to give thanks for the fact that they had actually woken up to live another day. No thing was too small or insignificant. Even flushing the toilet (among those who were particularly observant) earned a prayer of gratitude.

The young girl who remembered these things was now a young woman on the threshold of marrying me, irretrievably pagan and brought up to be derisive and, indeed, even aggressive to all matters pertaining to religion. As a child my older brother told me how he, my mother and one or two of my sisters, were caught on a small shingle island during one of the Hutt River's flash floods. This was news to me, and I perked up at the thought of the muddy water chewing off bits of bank and dragging down trees. Now my brother arrived at the point of the story. At this moment of crisis my mother had muttered a prayer. So he says. It was hard to reconcile this act in a woman I'd seen sneer out the kitchen window at our very good friends, the Browns, dashing off to the local Catholic Church. 'Off to confess and wipe the slate clean,' she'd say.

So, early on, talk of religion with my wife-to-be and her parents induced a moody silence from me. Occasionally a frown if the subject showed no sign of abating. It took my father-in-law two weeks to find a rabbi who would marry us. And this was in good ole liberal New York. Finally, he found Bert Siegal who counselled us over cheesecake in a deli near Bertanoe's book store in the Village. He warned us that mixed marriages, such as ours, rarely worked. The silences lengthened until all that passed between us were the noises of our cake forks scraping on our plates.

Neighbourhood Wars in Belvoye

We married in the apartment of my wife's 84-year-old grandmother. She was a remarkable old bird. She spoke English without a trace of Russian accent, or hint that she had known another world other than her weekly bridge meeting with the 'girls upstairs' and trips to the corner deli. She had arrived in New York, one of several kids, the only one able to speak English and, therefore, the first one to get a job. She had worked at the same book-keeping job with the same firm for most of her life. She didn't think much of me, and she was probably right to be suspicious of this foreigner of uncertain means and less than certain prospects. I wore a slight beard in those days, and once I overheard her complain to my wife, 'I wish he'd shave that ridiculous thing off.'

It was July, and brutally hot as only it can be in New York. I remember riding through mid-town at rush hour in, a steaming carriage crammed with bodies, all of us speechless on account of the heat, and a harmless, kindly old face dropped near ours to offer me a nectarine. I went to take it as my wife refused it. The woman smiled at us both and looked from one to the other. 'No, thank you,' said my wife. Later, she said she was absolutely right to refuse. 'That nectarine could have been poisoned.' Apparently, that was the second most dangerous thing that happened to me on that trip in New York.

The most dangerous thing was a walk through my wife's old Brooklyn neighbourhood on Eastern Parkway. Her parents were Brooklyn born and had spent the early part of their married life rearing their children two minutes from Grand Army Plaza with its Arc de Triomphe replica and the start of Flatbush Avenue where, in the early 60s, a jet liner crash-landed, scraping along the tarseal in the direction of the Duckors' apartment building. I was slightly envious. My childhood was filled with pine trees and playing fields. I grew up in a house with a front lawn, whereas she had grown up in an apartment building – six storeys of brownstone with purple ladders in a snakes–and-ladders formation, on the fifth floor a small balcony as useless and pointless as a bow tie. Across the street, on the diagonal, lay Prospect Park and the Brooklyn Museum. Now my wife began to fill in the landscape with story. She said a rabbi lived below them and complained all day at the kids roller-skating across his ceiling. In winter, she built snowmen across in the park. She attended PS 241 and her mother ran a tab for her at a nearby diner where she sat up to the counter for her shake and burger.

A more impoverished scene greeted us as we emerged from the subway. There was a greyness where I had been led to expect colour, and a heat one usually associated with the tropics. The once-busy sidewalk was covered in rubble and glass. A few bad men slid by in cars, their faces turned in the window looking at us with interest. My wife didn't seem to notice them or the rubble strewn over the sidewalk, or the torn green awning flapping like a piece of skin over the entrance to her old apartment house. She saw what she remembered and it was left to me to point out the sinister intrusions – as well as the elderly couple sitting out on the sidewalk in deckchairs, gloriously indifferent to these scenes of abandonment, smiling joyful smiles as if they were sunning themselves on the deck of a cruise ship in the Caribbean. They seemed to be smiling out of habit rather than for any reason. The old Jewish neighbourhood had moved on, and the place of my wife's childhood had eviscerated to memory. There was nothing left. Even out at Coney Island where we went to look up old childhood haunts we found the Parachute Jump in a state of rusting abandonment. We had a hotdog at Nathan's because, she said, 'Nathan's were the best hot dogs in the world.' Why, Nelson Rockefeller used to drive out to buy a hot dog from Nathan's. I looked up to see a pimpmobile crawl past, and near Nathan's where the Surf Hotel was offering 'hourly rates' a white woman with dishwater-coloured hair folded her tattooed arms beneath her massive breasts and sourly bit down on her gum. My wife bit into her hotdog and closing her eyes she smacked her lips. But, really, it was just a hotdog and I had tasted better.

Still, this little trip through the old neighbourhood was

worthwhile because, like other emigrants on the point of departure, she saw that a life in the 'old country' was unsustainable. I told her she was headed for beaches and fresh air. I began to sound like a voice-over for a Department of Tourism campaign. In San Francisco, where we lived before marrying, the sharp delineations of place didn't attach themselves to me – largely because she didn't yet know my old neighbourhood. I was out of focus, half-understood and half-known.

Now that we were back living close to the neighbourhood of my childhood she saw me in a new light. She simply had no idea I was such a rugby nut until half an hour before an All Black test match she lost the car keys out at Makara. Now she saw the playing fields, the rectangular spaces I'd grown up in, its dry lamington textures and the dreariness of the newspapers. She saw other people who looked a bit like me, fair, tousled, unkempt (and not particularly caring). She heard people who sounded like me, with half-bitten sentences and drawn-out vowels. She walked the coastline under grey skies and soon developed the same horizon-searching gaze. The mysterious parts of me were now sourced and what had once been exotic was now disappointingly ordinary. She thought that New Zealand belonged to the elements, that life here was somehow 'outside of experience'. In bad-tempered moments she'd let rip a burst at this 'white-bread country'.

In fact, 'white-bread country' was hardly a new experience for her. In 1968, the Duckor family left Brooklyn for upstate New York. They passed up timeless brownstone buildings and a babel of street voices for country rock and mock ante-bellum houses with white columns and huge lawns and circular drives. She had experienced this, as a traveller might, that is to say it hadn't rubbed off on her. And just as my uniqueness had been emphasised in San Francisco, so too was hers in New Zealand – a foreignness coloured more by Brooklyn than by upstate New York, and possibly brewed centuries earlier in Russia and the Ukraine, deep inside the Pale Settlement, a dotted line drawn across nineteenth–century Russia designed to keep Jews in their place, away from the blue-eyed north, and distanced from the mercantile opportunities of the major cities. Furthermore, her muddy complexion did not call up blond-haired suburban boys in dad's car with the stereo turned up to the Eagles. At Shaker High she wasn't a cheerleader, but she turned out in a school production as a belly dancer in a Turkish harem. She was dark and shadowed, whereas upstate was all grass and light.

Other New Zealand girls I had known and gone to school with were 'upstate girls'. I knew them, I knew their background, their upbringing, had inhaled the same whiff of chlorine from hot summer days sprawled on the blistering hot tiles of the suburban pools across the country. I knew their good-sort pizza-making mums and their dads who grew serious before a game on the box, and I knew their smirking brothers. It occurred to me that I knew these strangers better than I knew my own wife. It occurred to me one day in 1993 to go back to my wife's Brooklyn neighbourhood, to source her tones and inflections, and so, late one August morning after an exhausting flight across the Pacific and a redeye LA-New York flight, I woke in my wife's old bed, her teenage bed, beneath – of all things – a fabric design of St Basil's in Moscow, with the sun streaming through the curtains and half alert to and half in wonder at the musical chiming ice-cream truck that had just entered Patroon Place playing 'Waltzing Matilda'.

One of the peculiarities of Brooklyn, the largest borough in New York, is the near-total absence of hotels. In the Yellow Pages I managed to find a listing for the Surf Hotel out at the beach where I had seen that woman with the tattooed arms, and another for the St George Hotel. A woman with a foreign accent answered and when I explained what I was after she sounded surprised, 'So you want to stay?' I did – the Brooklyn Heights location swung it – and when I asked how much she dilly-dallied before finally answering with what sounded very much like a question, 'Fifty dollars?' I started to give my name and contact details but she cut me off to say, 'That won't be necessary.'

Neighbourhood Wars in Belvoye

The next day I took the subway to the Clark Station, first stop across the East River, and the deepest subway in all New York. I stood on the platform, my eyes smarting at the grainy subway air, and felt an intense isolation from the busy surfaces of the world. I felt the cold seeping proximity of the East River. I followed the other disembarking passengers to the lift (it is the only station with a lift) and we were slowly hauled up from the ocean floor to street-level.

We ran out of the lift and scattered in all directions. I seemed to be walking more slowly than anyone else and felt conspicuously out-of town with my overnight bag. Unbeknown to me, the hotel sat over the subway station like a kettle warmer and I found its unwelcoming entrance around the corner. An unsmiling black security guard pointed me over to the desk where the woman I'd spoken to on the phone looked up from behind a metal grille. She must have sensed me having second thoughts because she said, 'I'll give you a key and you can see if you like it.' Then as one of the other hotel 'guests' came down the stairs in slippers, and I caught something lunatic in the unshaven face, the woman behind the grille said, 'They won't bother you.' I didn't ask after 'they'. I took the key and went up to investigate my room on the fourth floor. There was only one other 'guest' on my floor – a huge white man, ten doors from my room at the end of an exceedingly long corridor. I only ran in to him once, and he was as startled as I was, but there was time to note an untidy looking soul in his fifties, white shirt, black slacks, his arms filled with newspapers.

My room was the last one on the floor. A thin wall separated my bedhead from the ventilator shaft of the Clark Street subway. All day and night a noise like a turbine rumbled away. It didn't disturb me as much as the August heatwave smothering the city. In the *Times* I had read of people knocking down doors to the apartments of their elderly relatives and finding them upright in chairs staring at a flickering TV screen, their mouths open in death. My room had no air-conditioning and in raising the windows I had to weigh up the noise from the street against the benefits of the slow breeze that barely shifted the stiff brocade of the curtains. More disturbingly, I found a stranger's pubic hair in the white-tiled bathroom.

The next day, out at Coney Island, an old nut-brown sun-worshipping Jewish woman heard where I was staying and clasped a hand to her chest, 'Oh the St George, that used to be so beautiful. Have

Lloyd Jones

you been in the swimming pool yet, hon?' I couldn't imagine the hotel that I knew having a pool. 'Oh yes,' she went on. 'It's got an Olympic-size swimming pool. Ask *them* to show it to you.' Then she went back to her earlier refrain, 'It used to be so beautiful.' And when I asked her when that might have been, she said, 'Oh, hon, I'm talking about the 1950s.' She said it was a salt-water pool, the only one in Brooklyn like it, and at one end she remembered it having a waterfall.

The woman was in her seventies, and the whole time that we sat talking on the sand ('The best sand in the whole of the world and I've been to Miami beach but this is the best!') her ancient girlfriends lay with their still arms at their sides, eyes closed, faces turned up to the sun. Occasionally one of the corpses would butt in to ask a question ('Where you from hon?') or to agree with one of the others. They came alive when I started asking after my wife's old neighbourhood. One of them sat up and pointed a finger at me. 'Don't even think about going there. Dey shoot you in broad daylight!' No one said who 'Dey' was, but I figured I knew. The schwartzes. The blacks.

For the first few days I set myself a schedule. Each morning, anxious to escape the St George, I would grab a coffee and a bagel from a place across the road, then in a small lift crammed with office workers drop to the subterranean depths of the Clark Station subway. Twenty minutes later I climbed the Brooklyn Museum exit out to the sunny maples planted along the sidewalk of Eastern Parkway.

One rainy morning in the Brooklyn Library I discovered the St George pool as in its heyday, a favourite waterhole of Brooklyn's finest – the hallways leading to the pool that had so mesmerised the old woman out at the beach were of a 'kind of golden, bluish glass carved with mermaids, mermen, and beautiful fish'. There was also news of my wife's parachute jump out at Coney Island. Interestingly, it closed down the same year that the Duckors loaded a Chevrolet and left Brooklyn for good. There was more – the Parachute Tower designed for the 1939-40 World Fair was sponsored by the Lifesavers Candy Company. Plus, in August 1940 Mrs Ann Howard of Manhattan and Mr Arno Rudolphi of Brooklyn and the Bronx were married mid-air while seated in a parachute chair; the minister, wedding party and even a small orchestra were hoisted aloft for the occasion. And here was something else. Parachuting was a Russian invention! Early in the century, James Strong of the US Navy had watched Russians in parachute training but their 'free jump' method he found 'unacceptable'.

Later, the sun came out and I left the library and looked across busy lanes of traffic to the sidewalk where once I'd seen the two old

Jewish overstayers sitting in deckchairs smiling out at the ruin. The awning outside 25 Eastern Parkway had been repaired and the old apartment building now looked quaint and cared for. I crossed the road and started walking up the Parkway, an hour and a half walk that took me past lovely gentrified brownstones with irises spilling their hearts over iron fences to unexpected rural scenes where front yards planted with corn reached as high as my shoulder, to buildings abandoned, concrete stuffed in their doorways to keep out itinerants, and the weeds! Some rampant hormone saw them sprout woody limbs that strangled brickwork and reached inside windows. I walked past the Jewish Centre and a succession of black churches (outside the Philadelphia Church of Universal Brotherhood a brother wore a table napkin on his head and sprayed detergent over his car, letting a light rain do the rest), after which I entered a distinctly different neighbourhood.

There suddenly appeared bearded men in black Prince Albert coats, their faces pale as winter. In the windows were posters of a fierce-looking white-bearded patrician: this was the famous rebbe Menazchem Schneerson (I would later see him in the flesh). Here, I realised, was the neighbourhood where my wife had stayed with the orthodox Jews all those years ago. It appeared intact, even thriving, with banners strung across Kingston Avenue proclaiming 'The Moshiah [Messiah] is on the way.' I kept walking, and eventually passed out of this piece of old Russia and Poland as, once again, abandoned tenement buildings reared up, the sidewalks became congested with rubbish, the maples and elms planted along the sidewalk looked sick and scruffy, some with their trunks covered in graffiti. The sense of leaving one neighbourhood for another was as palpable as any border crossing.

A few minutes later, at Utica Avenue, the vibrant colours of Haiti intervened and I saw women with magnificent head-dresses of shining plastic fruit and heard the ever-present urban whisper of 'Any change, man?' I passed down Utica into the Bed-Stuy neighbourhood to footpaths lined with markets – portraits of Selassie and reggae tapes.

Back on the corner of Eastern Parkway I looked up and felt a small flutter of excitement such as a bird-watcher must feel at finding through the end of his binoculars a rare feather – there, in among the neon of yet another Popeye fried chicken outlet, I detected the ancient words 'kosher' and 'cantor'. But two tablets don't make a mosaic, let alone a neighbourhood. The place of my wife's memories had no more weight and substance than the Russian mythical place of Belvoye – dreamed of, craved, celebrated, but undisclosed on any map.

In New Zealand I find myself constantly brushing with the landscape of childhood, tennis courts, playing fields (certain trees even hold special memories), whereas in Brooklyn I never sensed childhood, never so much as glimpsed it in the form of playgrounds or classrooms. In Brooklyn a more potent past was evident, one which went back to other countries and old arguments.

Tensions were still running high in the neighbourhood from an ugly incident two years earlier. Yosef Lifsh, a driver of a car in the convoy escorting the rebbe back from a visit to his wife's grave in the Old Montefiore Cemetery in Queens, had lost control of his car and jumped the sidewalk, crushing seven-year-old Gavin Cato against a window grate on President Street. It was undoubtedly a tragedy but a small one in a much larger epic. A black lay dead and a Jew was responsible. The driver was immediately surrounded by an angry crowd of blacks and beaten. Bottles were thrown, Jews chased and assaulted, while the blacks from the other side of the Eastern Parkway 'border' shouted, 'Get the Jews out' and 'Heil Hitler.' Later, a visiting Australian hassid, Yankel Rosenbaum, ironically in Brooklyn to study European anti-Semitism, was met head on with a crowd chanting 'Kill the Jews' and knifed to death. Local black leader Sonny Carson talked of liberating 'the community held hostage by a minority [the Jews] who have permission from the city authorities to do what they do with arrogance'. It was an old riff with a new spin. Hadn't the Reverend Herbert Daughtry once exhorted a screaming crowd to 'get the Jews and the people in the long black coats'? The black newspaper *City Sun* had run a two-part series on how Jews were responsible for the slave trade. And way before then, in Jewish communities across the Ukraine, Russia and Poland, the chant was 'Let all Zyhyds be massacred! Death to the Jews!' Following a nasty series of pogroms, a visiting delegation from Odessa was told by the Russian Minister of the Interior, 'We shall make your position so unbearable that the Jews will leave the country to the last man.' Nearly a century later his echo was being heard in a different country.

I'd been in Brooklyn Heights more than ten days now. One morning I woke at the St George suddenly alert to all its failings – the groaning beast behind my headboard that lived in the deep cataclysms of the Clark St subway and the heat which I'd come to detest like the worst of enemies. The newspaper hermit along the hall was also beginning seriously to spook me. Every time I passed along the hall I heard his door open and close behind me. It didn't help that for bedtime reading I'd been reading Isaac Babel's description of a night he spent billeted in a ransacked Jewish hovel. The great Russian writer finds the closets turned out, a human turd on the floor and a disembowelled featherbed which he takes for himself. In the night he is woken by a pregnant woman who tells him he's been kicking in his sleep and disturbing her father. When Babel pulls back the blanket on the sleeping man he discovers a corpse with his throat torn out.

    The Romanian woman on the desk reacted with horror when I told her I was moving out. 'But why?' she asked, and when I told her I was desperate for air conditioning, at least a fan, her head rocked back as if to say why hadn't I said so earlier. She chased after me waving a key to another room but it was too late. I had my heart set on another dump.

    The Carter in mid-town was even cheaper than the St George. It was a dump but at least it was a well-patronised dump. Low life and transsexuals from the all-night bar next door milled with foreigners

Neighbourhood Wars in Belvoye

looking for the cheapest night in Manhattan. There I carried on reading Babel's journey through the frontier towns where 'boys in long coats to their ankles still trod the centuries-old road to the Hassidic cheder'. The same figures I found crawling up and down Eastern Parkway. The same faces from Babel's frontier towns and my wife's childhood in black frocks defying the heat. While I might wander through their neighbourhood I couldn't really say that I entered it. The closed faces did not acknowledge me. Nor did the side streets brim with open doorways. Although I did enjoy walking along these leafy streets. The atmosphere was almost pastoral and this in a neighbourhood with frontiers delineated by rubbish and broken glass.

One Saturday morning I fell in with a young hassid on his way to the Lubbavich temple. Dorf was a Londoner. Recognising that we were both outsiders gave us that much in common. He invited me to attend the services. I didn't have a yarmulke but someone scrambled around on my behalf and found a plumber's cap. And so forty minutes after leaving the Carter in mid-town Manhattan I found myself descending the steps to a concrete bunker and from there a narrow door gave entry to a crowded hall. Dressed in a t-shirt and the ridiculous plumber's cap I went from street temperatures in the high nineties to a chill factor near freezing. For the first time I looked enviously around at the black coats.

The din was extraordinary. It was more like that of a marketplace than the solemn piety I imagined to inhabit such places. It was like biting down on something that you have never experienced before. Accordingly I rushed to judgement. Jews were short. Fat. Then a tall one with a learned squint brushed past. Succeeded by a squat one with a corrupt face. A comically fat one. Then a tall young man with Nordic features, a flaxen ponytail and cold blue eyes. Around me I heard Yiddish, Brooklynese and Russian. Old men with yellowing beards, younger ones, tall, distracted, averting their eyes. Upstairs, behind a window filmy with condensation the beautiful pale faces of the hassidim women – separated to prevent the subversive creep of unholy thoughts.

Dorf said I had 'lucked out'. Today they were celebrating the birth of the rebbe's father: he named the Ukrainian birthplace, a small village halfway between Kiev and Odessa to the south. Up at the front of the temple a group of bearded men pored over the Torah and mumbled a reading that could not be heard. Others shouldered by me. A small, shabbily clothed man with a grey beard tinged with green shook with rage while alongside a towering man half his age repeatedly apologised, 'I am sorry. I am very sorry.' I strained to hear more. The tide picked me up and carried me closer but by now the old man had switched to another language. Despite the noise and jostling the pious rocked back and forth and clasped prayer books to their chests. Bags of sweets flew through the air. Dorf said the sweets were to celebrate someone's marriage or another's bar mitzvah. A hand might intercept a bag of sweets meant for another, and in this way that person became part of someone else's celebration.

Every so often a chant went up in one section. I learned it was 'May our teacher, our master, live forever.' Young beautiful faces searched out their husbands through the shifting condensation. I was looking their way when a voice turned me around. 'I understand you are interested in the riots. What can I tell you? We're ten thousand Jews surrounded by one hundred thousand ...' Here the young man gathered himself and smiled, able to say it after all, 'Niggers.' This was a rabbi's son whom Dorf had sent over to speak with me. He described the 'protective pigmentation' of the rioters and the criminal background of the pogromshchiki (leaders): 'One is a convicted felon, another is a convicted kidnapper and murderer. Another is a disbarred lawyer.' Then another memory stalked across his face. 'Did you hear about Anthony Grazzioci? He was pulled from a car and shot dead. Why? Because he happened to look Jewish.'

I left briefly to warm up, and in a recess off the bunker I found a thin young man in long black side-locks muttering his prayers an inch away from a water-stained wall. He stopped when I stumbled in.

I apologised for the interruption and he shrugged which developed in to a smile. 'You are with Dorf?'

'Yes,' I said.

'Dorf is a good man.' He hesitated before asking his next question. 'You are from?'

I told him and he said, 'Ah yes, yachts. I know all about where you live. All you have to worry about is which way the wind blows in order to set your sails. A wonderful life.' But the way he said this indicated that it wasn't a life for him or even one to envy. It was how *other* people lived.

Back in the main hall the singing and chanting had started up again. Dorf showed up at my side shouting, 'How are you enjoying it?' At the approach of noon when the rebbe usually made his appearance, the chanting became more feverish. From the bleachers a man trained a pair of opera glasses on a curtained area at the end of the hall. Several times a teasing movement in the red curtains caused a new wave of hysteria to sweep the hall. Behind the curtains was a small room which had been built to accommodate the rebbe since his recent stroke. He could no longer walk and Dorf said no one had heard him speak for 18 months. As Dorf was telling me this a movement swept the hall and the congregation turned as one to face the east wall and mumble something. Then as the crowd turned back the curtains began to shift and a chant got up, one that was more vigorous and passionate than anything heard earlier. The rebbe appeared. It was the same face I'd seen in the posters lining the windows of Eastern Parkway – white-bearded, stern, charismatic.

'Look. His eyes are moving!' shouted Dorf next to me. And it was true – you couldn't look past his eyes. The rebbe's eyes were overloaded with everyday aspirations, as though with the wasting of his body all his energy had decamped to this last, small but spared area – like the Lubavitchers themselves, digging in around Crown Heights around the time my father-in-law had packed the car and left for a better career opportunity in upstate New York.

The rebbe's performance lasted only a couple of minutes before the red curtains were drawn, the hysteria subsided and the congregation began to filter out to the street. Outside, I was aware of a dumpy young man leaning against a fence paling and watching me. This was Yanky. He also knew Dorf. We talked about the riots and once he interrupted himself to point to the yellow line running down Eastern Parkway: 'We call that the border.' In Crown Heights the Pale Settlement of the Old World had been resurrected. Yanky described an eight-block area running from Eastern Parkway down to Leiffitz Avenue and from Nostrand Ave to Utica where the Lubavitch Jews lived. Outside those perimeters was a sea of black communities. Lubavitch takes its name from a small village squeezed between Poland and Russia. What was remarkable was how the border influences of the Lubavitch community in Crown Heights mirrored the Lubavitch in Europe. The borders of both communities were flexible. Lubavitch changed hands with every war, sometimes it was in Poland, sometimes in Russia. It had been fought over and survived pogroms. And in Crown Heights the Lubavitchers had seen off similar assaults.

Each night, Yanky said, he and the Neighbourhood Defence patrolled the boundary streets looking to surprise would-be thieves from the Bed-Stuy area. 'They all come across at night. We have blacks in our neighbourhood and they never give any trouble. It's the ones from over there.' He went on to say that over the past month there had been a run on car stereos and tonight they were going to 'plant' a car. 'You know, like tying the goat to the tree to catch the snake.' I thought I might like to see this, and he quickly agreed to the idea. Then he said, 'Call me around midnight.'

Saturday night. I sat on the edge of my bed staring out the window at the clock on the side of the *New York Times* building. My window gave on to the street where the trucks loaded up with the monster Sunday edition of the *Times*. Some of the drivers wandered across the street to buy a handful of counters and peek at naked girls in booths. Others got into shouting matches with the queens running in and out of the front door of the Carter. Around midnight, I walked down to Times Square and rang Yanky. I could just make out the voice at the other end. It was Yanky's brother. Yanky was already out on patrol but he'd left a message: he'd pick me up at 2am outside an address on Eastern Parkway.

It was forty minutes before a Brooklyn train showed up at Times Square. I sat next to a Haitian man dressed in an old-style three-piece suit. Balanced on his lap was a wedding cake. He'd just come from his son's wedding over in New Jersey. For the last two hours he'd travelled the subways carrying his portion of his son's wedding cake home. We chatted away about the wedding and Haitian politics, and got off at Kingston together. At the top of the steps he said, 'You take care now,' and proceeded across the border area. I found Yanky's address nearby and when I stopped I could still hear the footsteps of the man with the wedding cake trail off into Bed-Stuy.

But where the hell was Yanky? I shouted up at a lit window. A short moment later the sash was raised and a hushed voice called down to say that Yanky was on his way. A few minutes later, a Lincoln Continental pulled up. Its doors flew open and a number of young hassidim spilled out. One of them, someone's cousin, had driven down from the Canadian border to lend his car tonight.

I piled in the back of a second car and we followed the Lincoln Continental to its chosen park and picked up its driver. For the next hour we drove around the streets, deeper and deeper inside the shtetl. Yanky slowed down to stop outside a small house with a porch set back from the sidewalk. 'See that house? Last year a woman returning home with her groceries put down the sack to get the key and was raped and had her throat cut.' We drove up other streets past other landmarks with horror stories. Sometimes he gave our position to another car through a shortwave radio hook up. Finally, around 4am there was a burst of static and an excited voice reported a sighting near the planted car. We burst forward, up a sidewalk and shot down an alley behind a row of apartments. I saw a cat dart along a fence top. Then Yanky cut the engine and lights and we free-wheeled in the dark to the end of the alley.

No one spoke. The three of us in the back leaned forward. We rolled out the end of the alley into the street and there was the Lincoln Continental and there was a black guy by the driver's door. He looked up and we watched him discover us. Then very calmly he picked up his sack of tools and in his slinky singlet and hi-tops moved quickly up Brooklyn Avenue for the border. We trailed him; he kept looking over at us. Yanky radioed the other car: 'Red bandana, thirty years old. Isn't he the same guy we got last Saturday night? Well he's gone now. But he'll be back, the asshole.'

4am. One by one the vigilantes drop off until there is just Yanky and his brother left. It's been a quiet night. They half apologise. They explain that Friday night is the big night because the thieves know the Jews can't drive for religious reasons, and so on Friday nights the thieves from the surrounding countryside back themselves in a foot-race.

I sat back and closed my eyes to think about what I knew. Even the liberal friends of the Duckors who were from this neighbourhood accepted its decline as they might the passage of the seasons, as something inevitable and blameless. On the subject of their shift upstate, the Duckors' talk would resort to the code used to explain similar dispersals to the suburbs in the late 60s. The arrival of 'new elements'. Drugs. Blacks. My father-in-law's practice was struggling and the offer of a judge's position upstate was tough to refuse under the circumstances. But the real clincher came down to the little-admitted fact that the high school my wife was zoned to go to was seventy percent black. The Duckors are anything but racist. My father in-law had worked for a black law firm at a time when that option was far from fashionable. My wife's mother was in at the ground floor of the Head Start programme, a Kennedy initiative designed to give black kids a taste of middle-class life and values. However, despite the best of intentions, when their own flesh and blood was at stake the Duckors could not commit to the experiment. So they fled for Albany where my father-in-law says he couldn't sleep at night for the bird noise, and where, during the day, my wife and her brothers fossicked for Indian arrowheads in the un-landscaped area at the back of the house.

It's 5am and I'm sitting in the back of a taxi driving across the Brooklyn Bridge for the city. My eyeballs are hanging out of my head. I don't know what to think. I don't care. We drive along the canyons at dawn, the night's revellers spilling out of nightclub doorways, sleek women accompanied by carefree guys laughing, each with a beer bottle in their hand. It's hard to believe that we were in the same city tonight and I find that depressing. I think, why don't Yanky and Dorf and the rest of them get a life? Join a tennis club, learn to sail – and yes! care, despair even at a sudden wind shift as they hold the rope of a mainsheet in their teeth.

The next day (or is it the same day?) I'm on the D train rattling through Brooklyn's back yards for the beach. Across the aisle a coffee-coloured child with tight blonde curls, dressed in sharecropper overalls, is asleep in a pushchair. The child's handsome Russian mother in a yellow headscarf has the window seat. Beside her, a black mother-in-law, large, self-possessed, hips bursting out of a pink jumpsuit. Every so often she inclines her head to catch the words from this Russian woman-who-married-her-son. The Russian woman's father holds down another seat, a beach umbrella between his legs, eyelids closed, a smile attached to the gentle rise in his belly, inwardly rejoicing at how well things have turned out.

This is how it is. Somehow, and in spite of ourselves we fall across seas, continents, into each other's arms, surprised at first, then kind of liking the way the foreign bits come around to our touch.

I wonder what the black woman thought the first time she gulped down the vodka. And the Russians, did they separate the shredded coconut from the chicken pieces, thereby embarrassing the bride?

A Passion for Travel

I look out the window at the Greenwood Cemetery filled with those from the old neighbourhood. Lowensteins. Prusacks. Father. Wife. Siblings. All with a polite word for the world they have passed through; angels and lute-players pirouetting along the tops of the headstones with theatrical gestures and joyful speeches for the next world. The departing view is of cemetery workers, all of them black, some works vehicles, a grader, one or two of the men smoking and staring up at the rush of the train windows. One holds my eye – then he too is gone.

The
Last
I Saw Time
Paris

Joy MacKenzie

ON THE EUROSTAR from London to Paris an Englishman gave me an apple. He was travelling with his mother, a well-dressed, anxious-looking woman. Men who are good to their mothers generally make agreeable travelling companions. This man was reassuringly kind and eager to share his considerable knowledge of the City of Light. I listened to him discussing their itinerary: 'Palais de Versailles tomorrow. If we start out early we can take in the Royal Apartments, as well as the formal gardens and those wonderful fountains.' Obviously, he was a seasoned traveller who knew Paris well. I, on the other hand, knew Paris only from books, beginning with Ludwig Bemelman's Madeleine: 'In an old house in Paris that was covered in vines lived twelve little girls in two straight lines... the smallest one was Madeleine.' The Eiffel Tower, Nôtre Dame or place Vendôme was always there in the shadowy background. Later, Paris came to me from the pages of Jean Rhys's *Quartet*, François Sagan's *Bonjour Tristesse*, Anaïs Nin's *Henry and June* and Gertrude Stein's *The Autobiography of Alice B Toklas*: 'And so life in Paris began and as all roads lead to Paris, all of us are now there, and I can begin to tell what happened when I was of it.' Katherine Mansfield went to Paris seeking a cure from the Russian specialist, Ivan Manoukhin and wrote 'Je Ne Parle Pas Français', a story about that 'true Parisian', Raoul Duquette who, like all Parisians, lived 'in a state of more or less physical excitement'.

    I thought my furtive surveillance of my fellow travellers had gone unobserved, but the good-natured Englishman was aware of my nosiness. He said something to his mother and they both smiled at me. The good thing about travelling by train is that you can spy on other passengers reasonably discreetly. Your window becomes a convenient mirror reflecting the occupants of your carriage. Of course, gliding along at 140 kilometres an hour beneath the English Channel there's not a lot of scenery for you to pretend to be admiring.

    'Aren't you worried about all those tons of water on top of you?' said Don, my son, who lives north of London and was generously shouting me this trip as a special birthday treat. I hadn't really considered the weight of the ocean. Opened in 1994 by Queen Elizabeth and François Mitterand, the Chunnel was simply the fastest way of getting to Paris for an extended weekend. The Eurostar Express takes only nineteen minutes under the Channel: in less than three hours you've travelled from Waterloo station to Paris. You leave London, pass through green fields and hedgerows of merry old England and emerge into the sunny French countryside dotted with hay rolls, barns and tiny villages surrounding their central church spire. One stop en route at Calais to pick up passengers bound for Paris and you're there in next to no time. Quick, comfortable and very civilised.

In the buffet car I was dithering about what to order, when the pleasant Englishman told me that the patisseries were superb. I ordered a hamburger and a chocolate bar, but greatly appreciated his recommendation. After lunch, he said, 'Mother and I have some very good apples. Would you like one? I always take apples when travelling. Very often you can't get decent fruit.' I grew up with apple trees in the back garden and nothing beats new-season Golden Delicious but I agreed with him that these English apples were indeed very good. Probably *les pommes français* are just as delicious. The last I saw of the nice man was our mutual descent at Gare du Nord, when he was assisting his mother with her numerous pieces of floral tapestry luggage. Obviously, she was not a seasoned traveller. Seasoned travellers travel light.

I lugged my bag along the platform. So here I was in Paris – where it sizzles. Henry James called Paris 'the greatest temple ever built to material joys and lust of the eyes.' Where was the Eiffel Tower? I expected it to be looming above me, blinking a red welcome like Auckland's Sky Tower, visible from wherever you stood. But I didn't see it from the station. And I didn't see it from the taxi on the way to the hotel. And it was certainly nowhere in sight from our hotel in the 20th arrondissement just inside the city boundary.

My last trip to the UK (which was also my first trip) was in 1995 when I was still married. My husband and I, that very royal phrase, were away together for a month, during which time we discovered that being together all day, every day, only accentuated our incompatibility. In fact, we didn't seem to like each other much at all. It wasn't helped by the fact that he's a nervous driver (especially on the M1) and I'm a nervous passenger (particularly when there are lots of trucks around). I'm also very bad at reading maps. We stayed with friends in Devon before travelling on to Italy. Our friend Frank, who's big, jovial and bearded, couldn't believe we'd come all this way from Down Under and weren't going to Paris. 'Jill and I go to Paris every year. Paris is the most romantic city in the world.' Jill became dreamy-eyed, and said 'Paris is ever so romantic, especially at night. It's pure magic.' Well, we never made it to Paris and parted company a month after returning home. 'C'est la vie say the old folks/it goes to show you never can tell.'

This trip to the city of romance was not with husband or lover but with my dear friend Dorothy, who had done a French course at night school a year ago and was keen to practise her French. My *parle-français* was acquired in the fourth form, too many years ago, in a class that tittered when the teacher spoke of the city of Brest. She was not a native speaker and our pronunciation turned out pretty appalling. Together, Dorothy and I made a passable attempt to use the language and managed to get by for four days.

We were aware of our limitations, however, and chose a hotel where (so the brochure informed us) English was spoken: the Hôtel Armstrong at 36, croix Saint-Simon, in Montreuil, not very central and a slightly run-down district populated by a mix of Asian immigrants and turbaned Muslims. Montreuil's only claim to fame, as far as I can make out, is a large fleamarket and a jazz club called Instants Chavires where celebrities come to jam. I wondered if Louis Armstrong had ever graced the place with his presence and whether our hotel's name owed anything to him. Hôtel Armstrong is clean and pleasant, close to the Metro and reasonably priced.

Eager to sample some genuine French cuisine, Dorothy and I

walked around for ages looking for 'a good place'. We settled for dinner at a Vietnamese restaurant which was fine, but this didn't feel like Paris at all. We were tired; we didn't know how much to tip so tipped too much (not realising that all restaurants must display 'service compris' on their bills, which means the tip is included). Everything seemed alien. And where was the Eiffel Tower?

Next morning we were ready to explore. But with only four days, where to begin? The Louvre, of course. The Metro at the Louvre welcomed us with reproductions of its famous artworks on the station walls.

There are several magnificent edifices in Paris which, although now accepted with affection and regarded as essential Parisian landmarks, generated much controversy at the time of their completion. In 1889 the Eiffel Tower was seen as 'useless and monstrous', and incited three hundred distinguished citizens (including Maupassant) to sign a petition to have it immediately removed. It has been called 'the giraffe' and 'the world's greatest lamppost'. Then there's the Basilique de Sacré-Coeur which one Parisian called 'a lunatic's confectionary dream': Zola called it 'the basilica of the ridiculous'. The most recent construction to stir up Parisian debate is the 21-metre glass pyramid designed by Chinese-born architect Ieoh Ming Pei and completed in 1990. One critic called it 'perfectly useless, expensive, inaesthetic, out of place and degrading to the surrounding architecture'. True, the shimmering edifice seems totally at odds with its surroundings, but it's magnificent with the sun shining on it and magical at night. Whatever you may think of it, it's a very clear signpost to the main entrance to the Louvre. Dorothy and I visited the world's three famous women: Mona Lisa, Venus de Milo and the Winged Victory of Samothrace, who was discovered in many pieces but has been carefully put back together again. Artists were seated at easels copying some of the masterpieces. Dorothy commented on the many statues of men looking down at their penises – it seems penis anxiety has been around for a while. In *A Moveable Feast* Hemingway reports Scott Fitzgerald's unease about his sexual adequacy, his fear that he was not quite man enough to satisfy Zelda. Hemingway took him off to the pissoir to check his equipment, assured him he was quite normal and advised him to check the male statues at the Louvre.

Lunch, courtesy of Hôtel Armstrong, was eaten on green chairs at the Jardins des Tuileries. French lawns and gardens are very manicured and the grass is for looking at, not for sitting or walking on. My soft black patent-leather shoes became covered in white dust. I had worn these because Parisians are chic and fashionable, and I didn't want to let down the side by resembling a common tourist. Besides, I'd read a few hints in the *Berkeley Budget Traveler's Handbook* which said to bring your 'nicest traveling clothes if you don't want people staring at your tennis shoes'. French people dress more formally than we do, and shorts are 'frowned upon and will certainly brand you a foreigner'.

I looked quizzically at Aristide Maillol's chunky neoclassical figures and thought of Henry Miller who described walking in the Tuileries and 'getting an erection looking at the dumb statues'. Described by the historian Taine as 'an open-air drawing room', the Tuileries have long been a pick-up point. Well-dressed respectable young women of the eighteenth and nineteenth centuries coyly flirted while promenading on the gravel paths (poorly dressed people were turned away at the gate). A woman sitting alone on a park bench is considered an open invitation to a Frenchman, to whom flirting is almost mandatory, a point of honour. Perhaps because we weren't wearing our best clothes, Dorothy and I were left to nibble our filled rolls in peace. After three hours walking around the Louvre we were probably oblivious to whether the man on the chair opposite was giving us the eye or frowning at our walk shorts.

We strolled along the rue de Rivoli. So many books, so many movies, so many songs about Paris. 'I love Paris in the fall.' This was September and the skies were as blue as those in a Magritte painting. We walked until our feet hurt and then we took one of those city bus tours to get our bearings. Despite the plush red seats and earphones it isn't the most brilliant way to see the city – you get caught up in traffic and the sound quality of the audio equipment's not great. The tour we took was called Paris Vision, but our vision was fairly limited. Once we were on our way I kept wondering whether the other side of the bus was getting a better view and eventually I changed seats – then wished I hadn't. We passed the obelisk at place de la Concorde where Marie Antoinette was guillotined. The Metro there was where Ezra Pound gained inspiration to write his famous Imagist poem 'In the Station of the Metro':

'The apparition of these faces in the crowd;/ Petals on a wet, black bough.'

The voice in my ear told me we were coming to the exclusive haute couture area. Grouped around the avenue des Champs-Elysées, along avenue Montaigne and rue de Faubourg St-Honoré were Chanel, Christian Dior, Guy Laroche, Yves Saint Laurent and Christian Lacroix. We were instructed to gape at the swanky Ritz Hotel where guests arrive in bullet-proof limousines and stay in rooms with a view through bullet-proof windows. Ernest Hemingway reputedly said that he hoped heaven would be as good as the Ritz and the hotel has a bar named Hemingway to his memory. The Ritz family sold the hotel to Mohamed al Fayed in 1979 – one hopes Diana and Dodi spent blissful moments behind closed doors before their untimely death. No mention of the Queen of Hearts on Paris Vision's recorded commentary. In fact, having just left London where the city, the whole country, was grieving their lost princess, it was hard to believe the tragedy had happened here in Paris just weeks earlier. Our taxi from the station took us through a tunnel where we felt certain, the accident had occurred. It was just another day in Paris.

Parisians seem unaffected by anything. Their reputation of being an unfriendly, aloof and irritable race is perhaps unjust. They're private people who live their own lives and appear unconcerned about the goings on of others. Just don't get in their way when they're hurrying somewhere. Don't hesitate at the turnstile in the Metro and don't ask them stupid questions in very bad French. I asked an attendant in the Louvre where the Millets were and got a frosty reply. Wrong museum.

The bus took us past the Musée Rodin where we caught a glimpse of *Le Penseur* in the garden, showing off his muscles. In Rodin's words the thinker 'thinks with every muscle of his arms, back and legs, with his clenched fist and gripping toes'.

Traffic was bad as we approached the Arc de Triomphe. Some time ago, I saw a television programme which showed François Sagan perilously driving her red sports car here. I thought of Lucy Jordan's sad birthday when she laments the lack of this experience:

> 'At the age of 37 she realised she'd never ride
> through Paris in a sports car
> with the warm wind in her hair.'

As for me, when I was 37, I was deep in domesticity with three children and Paris far from my horizon.

Paris has always honoured its artists. When Paris Vision dropped us back at rue de Rivoli I noticed that the little shops were crammed with postcards of portraits of artists and their works. I sent Iain a postcard of the dwarfish Toulouse-Lautrec who loved women, especially women of the night, and, unlike certain American writers, had no hangups about his anatomy. I bought a card of the young Pablo Picasso outside Bateau-lavoir, 13. When he painted Gertrude Stein's famous portrait, she was not pleased, protesting that she looked 'nothing like that'. Picasso replied, 'You will.' And apparently, before long, she did.

Provided you're wearing good, comfortable walking shoes, Paris is a very easy city to explore on foot. Walking beside the Seine along quai des

The Last Time I Saw Paris

Tuileries, we crossed the Seine at one of the thirty-two bridges (I forget which) and wandered along quai d'Orsay in the pale late afternoon sun. Unsmiling well-dressed Parisian women trotted briskly past two flagging female tourists (one with the white dust of the Jardin de Tuileries on her black patent-leather shoes). We were on a mission to find the Eiffel Tower. Although we were in sniffing distance, we decided to pass on Les Egouts, the sewers of Paris, made famous by Victor Hugo in *Les Miserables*: 'All dripping with slime, his soul filled with a strange light.' People actually queue to go down these malodorous tunnels where they can see smelly water swirling around. There is said to be a good film which relates how three million baguettes, a thousand tons of fruit, a hundred tons of fish and so on make their way through Parisian stomachs and end up here. As well as sewer rats, some peculiar things have turned up in the system: an iron bedstead, the skeleton of an orang-utan and a piece of Marat's winding sheet.

It took a little longer than expected but eventually we crossed the avenue de la Bourdonnais and voila! Gustave's magnificent rose-coloured structure of filigree pig iron came into view. Dorothy and I bought ice-creams and joined the queue of tourists dressed in typically un-Parisian fashion: shorts, jeans, and *les baskets* (running shoes). We caught the double-decker lift to the top viewing platform (what else, although Dorothy confessed her palms were damp!) The view was magnificent. It was sunset and I wished my lover was beside me instead of my best friend.

It was a beautiful, clear, autumnal afternoon and we could see forever – well, at least fifty kilometres. With a few hundred tourists, we watched the sun go down and I thought, yes, it is true, Paris is the most romantic city in the world. I thought of Vita Sackville-West, disguised as a wounded sailor, leaving her Bloomsbury circle and dashing across the channel for a passionate weekend with Violet Trefusis. I thought of Héloise and Abelard lying side by side in the Père-Lachaise cemetery not far from our hotel. Of Napoleon and Josephine, Anaïs and Henry.

Dorothy and I were silent. I knew she was missing her Henry Miller-type lover and I missed my cuddly man. I sent Iain a 'wish you were here' postcard. And meant it. I also sent him a postcard with a little drawing of Saint Augustin (whom he admires) with a quote from *Confessions*:

'La mésure de l'amour, c'est d'aimer sans mésure.'

There's a superb restaurant in the Eiffel Tower called the Jules Verne, which is booked out months ahead. There's also a very good brasserie, Altitude 95, where Dorothy and I decided to eat. We both had delicious tenderloin beef, a glass of fine white wine, and a lovely French dessert – chocolate pear in brandy and cream. Food, service, view and ambience were absolutely unbeatable. At a table, across the way, a Frenchman smiled at me. This was the life.

There was just one little problem having dinner in Gustave's flagpole (Eiffel's own description), and that was the mad crush of people waiting for the lift back down again. The cologne-scented Frenchman appeared at my side and asked where I was from. He also asked whether I spoke French, but soon discovered that my 'un peu' was, in fact, almost 'rien'.

'Ah, la Nouvelle-Zélande. How did you get here? By canoe?' It was hard to tell whether he was teasing, baiting or flirting with me. In the lift we were jammed indecently together. When I was finally released from this not altogether unpleasant experience (the scent of French aftershave was in the air), he gave me his business card, which said he was a chef. 'Au revoir, la Neo-Zélandaise. Call me,' he said and smiled showing all his fine teeth. Of course, I didn't. Non, je ne regrette rien. In Paris, wrote Irwin Shaw, 'everything begins and ends at a café table'.

The mood of Paris had infected me and I felt like singing on the way to the Metro. A few complications getting home – too much French wine or excitement for one day and Dorothy and I went to the end of the line. We got out at Marie de Montreuil instead of Porte de Montreuil and found ourselves in an alien place, outside the periphery of Paris. We wandered around in the dark feeling like two lost souls. A black taxi cab came along, I hailed it, and we were happy to be driven back to Hôtel Armstrong where we were greeted with a solemn 'Bonsoir'.

24th September '97

Hello love,

I keep seeing happy Chagall couples flying away together. Today we went to the Château de Versailles. On the way home in the Metro, two undercover cops arrested two thieves – drug addicts covered in needle scabs – right under our noses. A big struggle took place. We just got out of the way in time. I'm ready to come home now.

Love,

Joy.

Queues don't bother Dorothy and me because we've always got plenty to talk about. In fact, I don't remember having an uncomfortably long wait anywhere. Inside the Château de Versailles, however, the crowd was a larger crush of bodies than we considered comfortable. We were swept along through the Grand Apartements into the Galerie des Glaces (Hall of Mirrors) and Marie-Antoinette's bedchamber, where custom had decreed that anyone who wished to could watch the Queen giving birth, thus ensuring the royal babe could not be switched for another. At times the audience was so great, people stood on the furniture to get a good view. This particular crowd was starting to get to us so we escaped outside into the beautiful park – French landscaping in the extreme – and found a peaceful place to eat our lunch. Afterwards, we rode the petit train across the immense grounds to the Grand Canal past Hameau, the toy farm Louis XVI had built for Marie-Antoinette, where she loved to dress up as a shepherdess complete with perfumed, beribboned sheep. The Queen's idyllic existence was interrupted by the March of Women on Versailles when six thousand hungry women demanded bread. Whether the Queen really did say 'Let them eat cake' is uncertain.

Dorothy and Joy (right) share a reflective moment outside the Hall of Mirrors, Château de Versailles.

Next port of call after Versailles was Montmartre. We caught the RER and the Metro, getting off at Anvers, and we spent a pleasant hour strolling around the little streets where Utrillo and Toulouse-Lautrec painted. Then we took the little funicular to Sacré-Coeur. Whatever one thinks of this wedding-cake cathedral, and whether or not you believe that the crypt contains Christ's sacred heart, seems immaterial. The view is what matters up here and it's awesome. We sat on the steps for a while listening to a busker playing his violin. Then we wandered down to a café where we stopped for a drink. Wine was $US3 a glass, Coca-Cola $3.50, coffee $6.50. It pays to drink wine.

While we were seated at our pavement table, an agitated young man came along and began cadging cigarettes from unrattled Parisians who responded by calmly giving him one, then lighting it for him, not blinking an eyelid as he continued to cadge, putting a few in his pocket for later. Lots of handshaking, muttering and loud exclamations issued from the madman. A sudden gush of soapy water burst from the gutter, and he washed his face and hands in it. Across the road the fruit shops displayed their gleaming produce and smart women hurried home.

Hi darling,

Our last day in Paris. Visited Edith Piaf and Oscar Wilde at Père-Lachaise, the city of the dead. What an astonishing place! Spooky, quaint, historical. We got there early so hardly anyone around. Just some pommy tourists looking for Jim Morrison.

People had placed flowers and chestnuts on top of Oscar's ostentatious headstone. Why chestnuts?

Home soon.

Love,

Joy.

On our last morning at the Hôtel Armstrong the big black waitress gave us funny looks. We ate a delicious breakfast as usual, and packed our lunch for eating on the Eurostar. But before getting the Metro to Gare du Nord for our return to London, we asked at the desk for directions to Paris's famous cemetery, Père-Lachaise. 'Take the rue des Orteaux and turn right down rue de la Réunion …' We walked and walked. Blow Parisian chic. We were now wearing our aerobics shoes. Mine, from The Warehouse, are the most comfortable shoes I own. Finally, there it was, beyond the mossy green pissoir, this unique necropolis, containing a million graves of writers, painters, composers, politicians, philosophers, singers, Resistance fighters, concentration camp victims, communists, rock stars and ordinary French folk. We had no idea of the scale of the place, over one hundred acres. With map in hand we walked in a flanerie (wandering aimlessly intent on missing nothing) along the cobbled avenues. All around us were tombstones, upright family mausoleums resembling stone sentry-boxes, elaborate sepulchres, stone cherubs, nineteenth-century ornamental sculptures and plastic flowers among beautiful old trees. No wonder we had difficulty finding some of the famous dead. We kept meeting a handful of tourists on a pilgrimage to Jim Morrison's grave. We didn't find it either, despite the fact that fans have been known to scrawl on nearby tombstones: 'This way to Jim Morrison.'

Chopin's grave is quite lovely with a sculpted angel and the branches of tall trees meeting overhead. He chose the site himself and even supplied some of the earth – Polish soil he brought with him in a silver box. His sister Ludwika, in accordance with his final wish, carried his heart back to Poland along with all the carefully wrapped letters he had received from George Sand.

Colette has a simple slab of marble – 'Ici repose Colette' – and, like Edith Piaf, she never lacks for fresh flowers.

Oscar Wilde's grandiose gravestone is dramatically different from its neighbours. Beneath Epstein's huge sculpture of a winged angel, donated by an anonymous female admirer, is a sign informing us that Paris City honours its dead and asks visitors to refrain from damaging the gravestones. Parisians are tolerant of (perhaps indifferent to) people's sexual preferences, but when the naked male angel was first raised above Oscar's burial plot, someone took exception to the erection and performed a castration. The head keeper now uses the stone penis as a paper-weight.

Gertrude Stein and Alice B Toklas (Lovey and Pussy, they called each other) lie together here; their names appear on either side of the same tombstone. Modigliani is buried with Jeanne Hebuterne, who, distraught at her lover's death, threw herself off a rooftop 'fino all'estremo sacrifizio'. Victor Noir, who was shot for criticising a relative of Napoleon III, lies on his back, his top hat beside his feet where it fell. Infertile women rub themselves against him hoping for a miracle.

There were several Paris experiences I would have enjoyed, given more time: a few hours at Musée d'Orsay, window-shopping along the Faubourg St-Honoré, a rhubarb ice-cream at Bertillion, a sidecar (my favourite cocktail) at Harry's New York Bar where it was invented, a peek into the Hemingway Bar at the Ritz, and lots of leisurely strolls around what is, undeniably, one of the most beautiful cities in the world.

But I was more than happy to have walked along the quais and to have seen the sun set from the Eiffel Tower. As George Sand said, 'I know of no other city in the world where it is more agreeable to walk along in a reverie ... Something in the air, in the "sound" of Paris, I don't quite know what, sways you in a way you won't find elsewhere'.

Safari

Catharina van Bohemen

A Passion for Travel

I'M SITTING IN the back of a jeep with my husband. We're being driven down a long straight road from the Victoria Falls airport to the Two Tusks Hotel. I hadn't wanted to come to Africa. I'm a solitary indoors person. I like to read: books about people who stay at home. Barbara Pym is one of my favourite authors. My husband Gerald read a book about evolutionary consciousness. I tried to read it, but we have different taste in books. 'I need to go to Africa,' he said. He discovered that you could do walking safaris. I like to walk. By myself. You can't walk by yourself in Africa, so tomorrow we're meeting strangers to walk in the hot, dangerous African bush.

The jeep travels slowly and stops for children who emerge from among sparse dusty trees, arms outstretched, or carrying polished wooden animals: hippopotami, lions, giraffes. Some arrange their carvings in groups across the dusty road so it's blocked by miniature mahogany hippopotami or monkeys. 'I give you good price, sir, madam,' others shout, thrusting animals into the jeep. No one buys. The lustrous colour of the wood glows against the children's thin arms and their faded clothes. They seem to expect rejection. They melt into the trees.

I stare at the soft lacy skin of the old American in his white nylon Kraft cap. His wife sits beside him. She's heavily built and wearing a slippery diamond-patterned dress with a deep vee. I see the crease between her breasts and there's a sweet powdery smell each time she moves. Her legs are swollen; knotty fingers grip the smooth curve of a walking stick. She wears a new pair of white trainers. 'Say, what do those deer signs mean?' she asks the driver, pointing at signs of leaping deer. 'Kudu, madam,' he answers. His eyes flash across his rear-vision mirror.

'We're hoping to see the Victoria Falls,' she says. Her husband murmurs, 'Yeah. And we're staying at the Victoria Falls Hotel. They say it's real English.' His small, even teeth click when he speaks.

I'd been looking at the trainers and the stick, wondering if they'd be on our safari. My husband squints in the hard white light. He sees a sign reminding the local people to keep behind the barbed wire – a legacy from the Zimbabwean war of independance. He nudges me. He puts his arm through mine, unclenches my hand and holds it. I look at the trees. A shiny white bus full of Japanese tourists overtakes us.

Victoria Falls township appears: the trees give way to open stretches of baked clay and corrugated-iron huts. Women carrying babies in embroidered slings, and holding toddlers' hands, glide along the road. Wicker baskets or cardboard boxes press down on their heads. They are mostly barefoot and walk alone, or with other mothers. Young men, pliant as reeds, their movements effortless, unencumbered, float beside them. They smile. Some sing. The sky is white, the sun invisible, the heat hard. Clouds of jacarandas throw blue shade over railway lines and scatter on the road like pieces of sky.

The jeep stops inside a gate framed by two crusty curving tusks. We gather our hand luggage. My husband smiles at the Americans. The driver unties our suitcases and Gerald pays him. In the lobby there's a raised pool in the centre with plants, the leaves soft and luminous after the dusty white road. I trail my hands in lukewarm water and watch Gerald and the man at the reception desk. His face is chiselled. He has a clipped beard and short tight curls; his skin is black and shiny. The sheen of his skin is counterpointed in the whites of his eyes and his teeth. He wears a fawn shirt and a glinting badge: Jimmy. As he speaks, he tugs his left ear lobe. His fingers are long and dark, the skin beneath his nails pink.

He punches numbers into a computer. 'You have come a long way. Welcome to Zimbabwe. The hottest time of the year. I see you are going on safari. An unforgettable experience. Very hot. Too hot for me.' He smiles. 'But you will see plenty of game. The end of the dry season, you see. All the animals search for water. In the meantime, sir, your room is 41 and we have a pool.'

We sit beside the pool. It's late afternoon and the courtyard is filling up with local families coming to swim at the end of the day. The dining room leads onto the courtyard, and from somewhere inside I hear 'The

Surrey with the Fringe on Top'. The buildings are low, single-storeyed, shabby. They remind me of a tearoom in Palmerston North where I once stopped as a child on my first trip to Wellington. Even the food smells like food I ate when I was ten.

I try to read but the music, the nickel teapots engraved with two tusks, and jugs of powdered milk bewilder me. Children throw cake to monkeys which leap and swing from surrounding trees with harsh red flowers but no leaves. The monkeys squeal stridently: one hoists her baby on her hip and with her free arm swings to the ground for more cake. A few moments later, she picks her baby's head for insects, which she eats.

'Which of these people will be coming with us, do you think?' Gerald asks.

'What about those two? They look as if they're waiting for something.' I nod towards two men who have moved their chairs slightly away from the families. Beer cans, cigarettes and potato chips lie scattered on the table in front of them. One man reads. He has thick red glasses; the book nearly touches his nose. A freckled hand strokes long pale legs. Occasionally, he reads something out to the other man who grunts or laughs. His skin is sallow and he has a patchy beard. His glasses are black beneath a military-green sunhat with flaps that cover his neck and ears. His beard bothers him. He rubs it and looks at his fingers.

'What if I'm the only woman?'

'What if you are?'

'Do you think that's the guide?' A small thickset man has walked into the courtyard. He's dressed in short faded khaki shorts and shirt. He's wears a wide-brimmed, sweat-stained canvas hat and a paisley scarf round his neck. His legs are brown and smooth. He has worn Reefs on his feet. He stands for a few minutes looking around and then opens a battered leather satchel. He gets out a dog-eared sheaf of papers and, after glancing at them, looks at the two men. He walks over and the men get up and shake his hand. A waiter brings whisky.

'Must be,' says my husband who walks over, greets them and turns and waves at me. The men watch as I walk. The monkeys' chattering grows shrill.

'This is my wife Rina,' says Gerald. 'She's worried she'll be the only woman.' He puts his arm round me. 'This is our guide. Leon. And this is Larry and Harvey from Los Angeles.'

The Americans murmur, 'Hi.' Larry with the red sunglasses says, 'We noticed you. We figured you'd be in our group. I could kinda sense your expectation.'

The guide looks at me. He doesn't smile. 'You're not the only woman,' he says. 'There's one from Perth. She's arriving tonight. And there's a Brit. He should be here.' Leon looks round the courtyard. He sighs. His glance suggesting impatience or resignation. 'Little to say, really,' he says. 'You're here to walk. We had New Zealanders on the last safari. Too hard for them. I suppose you can walk?' He looks at me again. I want to tell him I love walking, but I'm a solitary walker. His silent appraisal suggests doubt.

'Rina's a great walker,' says my husband. 'She loves it.'

'It's not hard,' says Leon.

The small bearded American called Harvey says, 'Oh, sure. We're really looking forward to it. We've been canoeing in the Okavango Delta. Be good to stretch our legs.'

'Yeah. Those dugouts sure are cramped, but the bird-life is really inneresting. I got some fantastic photographs,' says Larry.

'Little to say,' the guide repeats. 'Do what I say and you'll be safe. You'll need to sign these before we start.' He drops the papers on the table.

What is this?' asks Harvey, gripping the sheets and frowning. 'I was an attorney back home.'

'Just means if you're attacked and killed by a lion, or eaten by a croc, it's not my fault,' says Leon.

'Not worth anything,' Harvey says. 'We're covered for this kinda thing back home.'

'What about us?' I ask Gerald. He smiles and shrugs.

The Englishman arrives. 'So sorry I'm late. Got caught up. Birds, actually. Mark Mainwaring. I take it you're Leon? The guide?' He beams at Leon who responds with a tight smile.

Mark Mainwaring is tall, fair, confident. He has a long narrow nose with a fine red tip. He shakes hands with the men and glances at me. He's wearing khaki shorts and shirt but they're new, with sharp hard creases. He's carrying an identical hat to the guide's. A book about birds of Zimbabwe protrudes from his pocket.

'Departure times,' says Leon. 'These people,' Leon jerks his head, 'start tomorrow. Larry and Harvey from Los Angeles. Gerald and Rina from New Zealand.'

'The colonies,' Mark says to Gerald. 'We've got friends in New Zealand. They farm in Hawkes Bay.'

Leon continues, 'We've got a seven-hour truck trip tomorrow up to Chizarira. Leave here at six-thirty. Sharp. Zimbabwe time. Not British time. You're a British dip, aren't you?'

'For my sins,' says Mark.

I listen to Gerald's breathing. I don't want to get up early to drive into the bush with a laconic guide, a pair of ageing hippies and a supercilious young Englishman. The air is thick. Through the strange night sounds, I hear singing. Our room is next to the hotel laundry, a large airy space like orchard packing sheds. I heard singing when we arrived and followed it to the laundry where maids sang as they worked. When they saw me they stopped. They said the laundry was closed. I'd gone back to the pool, but I couldn't read. The monkeys racing across the roofs, the women's voices, their sudden silence, when they saw me, emphasise how near the other world is, and how separate. Now, in the middle of the night, men are harmonising with the women. I'm exhausted by the strangeness of sounds, smells, colours.

'Bring as little as possible,' the guide had said. 'My boys will wash your clothes.' Thinking about his boys reminds me of the children and their music lessons. I see the wall planner on the fridge. I fall asleep telling my son to empty his lunch-box and hang up his school bag.

A woman stands on the jeep's running board helping to lash suitcases to the roof, looping and tying ropes, shouting suggestions to Leon. She wears brown Lycra bike pants and an orange tee shirt with JUST DO IT printed on it. She has breasts like melons and round buttocks which ripple beneath the bike pants. She has muscly calves and a new pair of tramping boots. 'Worried about being the only woman?' Leon asks me. 'Meet Leonie.'

Leonie jumps off the jeep and rubs her hands on her hips before grabbing mine. She has a loud flat voice. 'Hi,' she shouts. 'Looking forward to it?'

'Not sure,' I say.

We drive throughout the morning. Leonie sits beside Leon. She leans her arm on the window. She looks as if she's always driven along these rutted roads. She bellows at Leon and points at people, pylons. I can't hear much except that the land looks just the same as home. The only difference is the animals.

Mark has stretched his legs over his pack and pulled his hat over his face. I sit between him and Gerald, and in the back seat the Americans lean against each other. A black man sits in the corner of the jeep. 'Agrippa, my tracker,' says Leon. Agrippa smiles but avoids our gaze. Everyone dozes, except me. I look into the rear-vision mirror. Leon is watching me. I lean against Gerald, but Leon's eyes still see me through the mirror tied to his door. His rifle rests between two hooks across the dashboard.

Metal roads merge into dirt tracks. The jeep is old and open with two rows of hard canvas benches. As its engine roars and whines, potholes and sudden dips hurl us together. Sometimes a bus or truck carrying women, bundles bearing down on their heads, and empty-handed men, pulls over to allow us to pass. The people in the trucks wave. The trucks are old, their paint chipped; numberplates, lights, mirrors are tied on with rope or pantyhose. Children, some carrying bags, trail along the road. 'Walking to school,' says Leon.

The landscape is hard, dry, featureless – stunted twisted trees, rocks, brown-baked hills which fold into purple mountains. The sky is a bright blue plate. Maize grows along the road. Round thatched huts, the same colour as the maize, are almost camouflaged except for a thin plume of smoke, or a corrugated iron door painted turquoise. Leon slows the jeep. A woman sits on the bare ground outside a hut nursing her baby. Her hair is hidden in a cotton turban, her skinny legs outstretched. A toddler stands beside her, hand on her shoulder. The mother looks at the jeep. The whites of her eyes gleam. She doesn't smile, but the toddler waves. Leon raises a finger.

Further along the road, a boy squats like a cutout beside piebald goats who pick at grass among the dust. The goat boy holds a switch and flicks it as we pass. Flies crawl round his velvet eyes. Under a rare tree with spreading branches and large leaves, men sit cross-legged. 'What are they doing?' I ask Leon.

'Waiting.'

Late in the afternoon, when Leonie's arm is scarlet, we climb into Chizarira National Park, one of the most isolated wildernesses in Zimbabwe. Chizarira derives from the Batonka word 'chijalila' which means 'closed-off' or 'barrier'. Herds of deer – impala or kudu – scatter as the truck clatters down to a bank beside the river Busi. There is no river, but a sandy emptiness where Busi will flow when the rains come. The bank is like a park – attenuated shadows of acacias stipple the ground. On the other side of the river, the land is broken and bony. Birds with shining red or blue feathers paint the sky. Here where the predominant colours are bleached or tawny, a bird's wing is a vivid flash. The size of Chizarira overwhelms me. I'm used to fences, walls, signs which divide and separate, but here the land unfurls endlessly.

The boys – men of indeterminate age called Stephen, Collett and Stanley – who arrived first, found and buried a dead buck, but the smell lingers. They've lit a fire and erected light grey plastic tents. They've dug for water beneath the sand. They talk softly to Leon in Shona, a low liquid language, full of tumbling 'lls' and 'mms'. We inspect our tents, each with two stretchers and outside the tents, small canvas basins with warm water.

'You're lucky,' Leon says. 'The boys have seen lion. Over there.' He points at a rocky outcrop about two hundred metres from the camp. 'They sit there in the mornings in the sun. At night, they look down at us. Don't wander off. Animals here are not used to humans.'

Harvey says, 'Ya mean we might, like, actually see a lion?' He licks his lips and scratches his beard.

Leon doesn't answer at once. 'Good chance,' he says.

We leave in ten minutes for our first walk. Leon tells us to fill our water bottles and gives us a safety talk. He takes off his hat and leans his rifle over his shoulder. Harvey's talking to Larry. Leon looks at Harvey until he's quiet. 'In the bush,' says Leon, 'you walk in silence and in single file behind me.' He tells us about the Big Five: lion, leopard, buffalo, elephant and rhino. He says they're called the Big Five because when they attack, they kill: 'If a lion attacks you, don't act like prey and run. Freeze until I tell you to move, and then run in the opposite direction to the attacking animal.'

'Poachers are the other danger. If we see poachers, we shoot. I'll use this if I have to and Agrippa will shoot if he has to.' I look at slim Agrippa with his shiny aubergine legs – there is a sore on one which weeps throughout the safari. When he smiles, his mouth is wide and pink with black spaces where teeth used to be. He has a small silver pistol in a leather pouch and carries a long thin stick. He's the only person who doesn't walk in single file. He drifts around in circles, prodding stones and dung, searching for lion tracks. Mark calls him Agrippa the Gun. He used to be a poacher.

'Any questions?' asks Leon.

'What do they poach?' I ask.

Leon sighs. 'Tusks, horns. Anything in the drought.'

We follow Leon across the dry Busi river and enter a place of black thorn trees. It's very quiet except for the birds and the gurgle of our water bottles. One bird says 'Crack'; another, which even Mark never sees, is the 'Go away' bird. Over the next few days I always listen for the go-away bird.

Leon is a rhythmical relaxed walker, despite carrying binoculars, water bottles, first aid. He wears his rifle slung across both shoulders, his arms suspended from it. He points to tortoises, the metallic blue dung beetle, birds for Mark, who ticks them off in his book. Leonie stumps along behind Leon. She has long sight, likes to spot game first and state their sex; 'Warthog. Female.'

Mark is pigeon-toed and lurches forward like a ship. He walks behind Leonie (I had heard him tell Leon he'd hoped to follow a curvaceous little bum round Africa). Harvey scuttles behind Larry whose white legs spring through the brown spiky miombo grasses. I walk behind Harvey. His head twists nervously and he flings thorn tree branches back onto my legs. Sometimes they swap places. Even though Larry is nearly blind, he anticipates every branch or spike, and holds them till I pass. Gerald is last. He has a video camera. When we come home, all he has to show of our safari is two minutes of twelve legs slicing through miombo.

Leon leads us down a deep gorge. We stumble and slip, scattering small stones. At the bottom of the ravine is a stinking black puddle raked by fingers of green slime. 'An old croc lives here,' says Leon. Huge rocks and boulders litter the floor of the gorge. On the baked mud floor among the rocks are bones, dung, the imprint of hooves, paws, claws. Leon points to the scattered remains of an elephant skeleton. 'Look at the skull,' he says. 'It's honeycombed, so it can bear the weight of its head.' It's silent, menacing, stinking down in the gorge. The light is fading, the rocks becoming black. I wonder how it feels to Leon to walk into a gorge and to know the bones will always be there.

Sudden shrieking shreds the silence. Baboons scramble over the rocks, running over one another cackling, stretching their lips, baring their teeth.

We climb back up the gorge and walk into a sheltered place where trees grow close together and the grass is longer. Leon stops and gestures to us to freeze. Twenty metres away three elephants are ripping branches with their trunks and cramming them noisily into their mouths. The elephants are thin; their skin hangs in grey hairy folds. Their ears flap. Leon points to a termite mound which we climb to get a better view. It's like spying: watching their concentration as they slowly move around the trees and then swing away into the darkness.

Leon whispers that elephants' sight is not good, but their hearing and smell are excellent: we're down wind of them. I'm exhilarated rather than frightened. Leon's knowledge of the bush is obvious. I've fallen easily into the pattern of walking with these strangers in the deep, hot silence.

We sit around the table beneath a thatched shelter, one of the few permanent facilities in the reserve apart from the round fly-infested holes ('Check for snakes,' said Leon) that pass for lavatories. We're clean – a tattered tent strung up around a nearby tree is our shower, where we crouch on a slippery plastic sheet to catch warm water from a bucket suspended from a branch. We've drunk gin and eaten a casserole cooked by the boys crouching over dented pots on a low fire. Leon's rifle leans against a post supporting the roof. He seems relaxed but his eyes continually sift the night. Lightning scratches the star-stapled sky.

'Look,' he says. The darkness is full of flickering outlines, thickening into clumps, shifting, dissolving. 'Buffalo,' he says. 'They like the fire. Look carefully and you'll catch their eyes.'

'I see them,' says Leonie.

'We might track lion tomorrow,' Leon says.

The men discuss their occupations. Gerald says he's a lawyer but thinking of giving it up. 'I read a book called *Beyond the Human Condition*,' he says. 'It's about instinct and knowledge.'

'You mean attorney?' says Harvey. 'I used to be an attorney. I gave up.'

'I read anthropology,' says Mark. 'I wish there were still countries to discover. This safari is frustrating. We get up in the morning and walk in a circle. I want to discover. I wish there was a tribe left, even a small sub-tribe.'

'At least you've got birds,' I say. 'Have you heard of Barbara Pym?'

'I have,' says Leon. 'I run a second-hand book shop back at the Falls in the wet season. I collect stuff by Stanley and Livingstone. Sometimes Barbara Pym comes in. I like to read.'

Larry doesn't say much. He leans back in his chair, one pale leg crossed over the other and peers at us through his red glasses. When Leon asks him what he does, he says, 'Property. Venice Beach.'

Leon tells us he was in the Rhodesian Army. He tells us about Operation Egg. 'They dropped you in the bush with an egg and the clothes you were wearing. You had to return to camp three days later with the egg, but it had to be cooked. Otherwise they smashed it on your face.' He said it was easy to find shelter and make a fire in the bush. He filled the husk of a magongo flower – about the size of a magnolia – with water, and boiled the egg. He ate crocodile eggs and magongo nuts. 'I can survive in the bush,' he says.

Leonie says her husband works on oil rigs and she only sees him for a few months a year.

'Why did you come?' I ask.

'A dream.'

'Did your husband want to come?'

Leonie looks at me. 'You can't share dreams.'

I lie on my stretcher and listen to them discussing marriage. Mark's the youngest. 'Should I try it?' he asks. 'Sure,' chorus the Americans. 'We've been married four times between us. Wives come and go. You do it for the kids.'

They ask Gerald how long we've been married. 'Amazing,' they say.

In the night I hear, among scratchings and whisperings, the roar of lions and a strange spine-chilling howl. Leon tells me it's hyaena. Gerald says Leon slept outside beneath the thatched shelter. His rifle lay beside him.

I wake to the metronomic tomtom of hornbills, the sting of cicadas, and Gerald saying we're going to track lion. We drink tea in the cool morning air. The beginnings and ends of days here arrive suddenly. In the mornings the sun races over the bush bleaching darkness, fixing the land in a hard bright stare. The light is golden and gentler at dusk.

Leon tells us to hurry – it will be very hot. He's almost excited. We walk away from the rocks back across the river bed. Agrippa isn't walking in his usual indolent circles – his stick twitches. He talks to Leon. 'Fresh tracks,' says Leon. Agrippa thinks the lion is dragging prey; he thinks it's a mother lion. Mother lions drag their prey to sheltered places. I try to remember what Leon said in the safety talk about not acting like prey. We almost run, but it seems to me we're walking in circles. The sun's heat is hard and heavy. Sweat slides down my skin. My head thumps, my glasses are steamed up.

I remember my walking meditation, but keep repeating, 'Breathing in, breathing out, I am calm, I am smiling.' I learned it from a nun in a saffron sari in a convent parlour. As she chanted, her coffee-coloured feet rose and fell on faded floral carpet. It was important, she said, to say the meditation slowly, to take your tempo from your body's breath. Outside tuis sang, dark rubbery leaves pressed against the open windows. Old women in stockinged feet walked round the room chanting in thin quavery voices: 'Breathing in, breathing out, I am calm, I am smiling. Present moment, wondrous moment, Peace to the world.' When I say the walking meditation at home, when I'm by myself, the muscles in my face soften, my fists unclench. Today I'm behind Harvey. His head swivels from side to side and his short legs almost dance in his efforts to keep up with Larry.

We stride down to a bend in the dry river bed. There is no lion, no mother lion dragging its prey. A fig tree, perhaps thirty feet high, grows out of a ledge of rock shaped like an altar. 'This is a sacred place,' Leon says. 'I often light a fire here and burn tobacco.' He points to brilliant red flowers growing on thick rubbery stalks in rock crevices. 'The nyangas use this flower to send them into trance,' he says.

Agrippa is downcast. He prods at some very white dung. 'Hyaena,' he says and his eyes flash. 'Hyaena eats bones.'

We return to camp slowly. Leon leads us through a thicket of shimmering mopani trees. Mopani means butterfly: the leaves are shaped like butterflies' wings. Young leaves are copper-coloured and joined. As they reach maturity, the leaves unfold to a pale, copper-shot green. They quiver in the sun's hot breath or 'when man disturbs the sacred silence of the bush.' Leon looks at me. 'Read Laurens van der Post?' he asks. 'Airy-fairy, but that's what he thinks.'

The boys laugh when we get back and tell us that the lions have been on the rocks all morning. They point to the rocks. Leonie says she can see three. A male with a black mane, and two lionesses. I look. I see only rocks. I'm short-sighted – I've studied dung because it doesn't move. Elephant dung is small round hay bales, buffalo dung the most beautiful – like black roses.

We eat and set off again and walk in circles again. It's the middle of the day – even the birds are silent. The ground shimmers. My head hurts. I want to go back to camp and read. I want to be out of the sun. I don't care about lions. I imagine myself floating above us, looking down on a frail human thread weaving among stones and bones.

Suddenly Agrippa shouts. 'Simba!' Everybody runs away in the same direction. Everybody except me. I freeze. I wait for Leon's order to run in the opposite direction to the attacking animal. I don't see any lions, I don't hear any orders. My heart is thumping, my headache has gone, I cling to the tatters of my walking meditation: 'I am calm, I am smiling'. I shut my eyes. I wait.

My husband bends over me. His face is glistening with heat? Excitement? Concern? 'What happened to you?' he asks.

The others appear from behind rocks. 'Did you see them?' they ask. 'We got some fantastic shots.'

'I'm freezing,' I say. 'I'm waiting for the order to move.'

That night at dinner, Leon says we'll be leaving tomorrow for Hwange National Park. 'No walking,' he says. 'We'll see more game but we'll be in cages. Nobody gets out of the truck. You'll get good shots of lion, but it's not the same as here in Chiz.'

Leonie, who's been popping her blisters, asks if anyone would like a massage – she does part-time massage in Perth and has lavender oil, but not much. Leon says she could mix it with some of the boys' cooking oil. Mark has a sore shoulder; Gerald wants a foot massage. They discuss cricket and Leonie kneads them with strong red hands. The Americans ask what 'underarm' and 'whingeing Pom' mean.

'It's a pity we haven't got an instrument,' says Leon, pouring thimbles of port. 'Music's good in the bush.'

'I've brought my recorder,' I say. Everyone laughs.

'Play it,' Leon says. 'I like English folk songs.'

I play Leon the theme and variations of 'Greensleeves'.

Larry says, 'Nice.'

After I've played, Leon pulls a magongo nut – small and hard like an acorn, from his pocket. 'To remind you of Chizarira,' he says. 'You surprise me. I'm not often wrong about people. I watched you in the jeep coming up here. Not one smile. Your mouth was a thin line. I thought, I don't have to like her, I'll just make her walk.'

Catharina van Bohemen

Grin *like a* Dog

Peter Wells

A Passion for Travel

THE NIGHT WAS hot and the heroin, which was flooding Sydney, has become cheaper than booze. I knew this because, a couple of days before, I had turned the corner sharply into my apartment building and was surprised by two winoes camped out on the porch floor. They greeted me – Australians are nearly always hail-fellow, well-met – and I returned their courtesy then got inside. It was only when I was behind the plate-glass door that I registered I had seen a spoon lying on the tiles. I looked back as I went up the stairs. I saw a needle being jabbed into a lard-white arm.

I live not far from Kings Cross. I can choose to go through it when I want to experience a millennial vision of Gin Alley – except the spirit of oblivion is no longer gin. I see Polynesian kids there – who have probably never been to New Zealand. Maoris. I see the elderly whore who is dressed as a matron, respectable, bespectacled, trim in high-heels. I see the junkie prostitutes with their needle eyes and pallid skins, as if nourished by flourescents and fed by the cold chips which lie in the gutters. I don't understand how anyone can find them attractive.

But Kings Cross, which became a sex-and-drugs venue during the R and R days of the Vietnam War, is the place men come to every Friday, Saturday night – as if to visit a shrine, practising their clumsy or hopeful mantras of sex, still persistently believing in the magical renewal of the act itself when all around them the evidence argues persuasively that the miracle has long gone.

Sometimes it's so hot and seedy that it feels like a forgotten suburb of 'Nam. As if by osmosis, what the Americans experienced, they brought – along with strains of VD – and smeared it all over what had once been a little jewel of bohemia. Now Kings Cross seems to have become something else – it has a kind of vegetative ambience, or rather it is like a spore which has spawned and spread and now covers everything in that district. Yet when I look at it, I can see other worlds too – I can see the eighteenth-century world of Hogarth's London, of teeming slums and al fresco sex happening in doorways. This, too, seems to segue into Sydney's past. It is as if the long hand of history, of whatever experience, is locked into genes and then manufactured through social custom. It's as if it reproduces its own world again, in a peerlessly new territory: and the heat, so undermining and sexualising, persistently reminds you that it is not, it was never going to be, a distant part of England. In fact, on still evenings, when the city waits for the resolution of a storm, it feels more like South America.

I've always thought that Sydney played Paris to our prosaic London (or Manchester, or Walford or whatever it is we are most unlike). By this I mean Sydney was the place you went to *sin*. It is the biggest wen we have in our Antipodes and as such it has an enduring allure for those who want to prove themselves against something bigger, or simply swap their mundane circumstance, shrug off the straitjacket of habit and become – for an hour, a few days or weeks – someone else. I know this because this is what Sydney was for me.

To a certain extent I came out in Sydney. I had my first adult sexual encounter there. I got fucked in Sydney. I realise this looks like something defiantly scrawled on a wall, and in a way it is. But I say it with a certain amount of insouciance, based on affection towards this accommodating old whore of a city. I had had a confused and constricted adolescence in my hometown of Auckland. By the time I was eighteen, I was a long-term prisoner of the closet. I was trying to fit in with my family's projection of me, which naturally, since my parents were both heterosexual, included my being straight. I couldn't be, of course. In my twenty-second year – by this time I felt very old – things changed.

I had a friend who lived in Sydney. He came out to me by letter. I flew over to see him. He showed me round town. It still embarrasses me to think of that night, my first adult sexual encounter. I was so defiantly young, so graceless. I remember I came very quickly and the man I had chosen to be the instrument for the loss of my recalcitrant virginity was not especially pleased. He had to drive me back to the nightclub where

I had presented myself to his slightly startled presence. That night I had the determination of the pilgrim arriving at the site of a mute oracle. But the following day I felt I had a secret cause for celebration. Each slightly awkward step seemed a walk into a new life. I knew, in whatever confused yet victorious way, that I had attained something. I had become a unified person. Sydney gave that to me, and for that I will always be grateful.

It has just occurred to me that I could only write what I've just written because I'm in Sydney. If I were in Auckland I would feel, almost subcutaneously, as if through the skin of my eardrums, that my family, my friends – even worse, my acquaintances – would be listening. Perhaps this is the greatest gift of travel – a vertiginous sense of freedom. I sit here in my room in Sydney and psychologically all I have around me is space, an ideal blankness – a lack of connection. In my own country, living in the town in which I grew up, the space at times feels minuscule: every road seems honeycombed with the passage of passers-by, all of whom I know by sight, or who know me. Or is every one of those passers-by myself in all my incarnations, babe, child, adolescent, young man, older man carrying the burdens, the weights of all of these invisible selves?

It is as if we carry with us all the patterns we have made when we live in a familiar city. This is the intoxication of being somewhere else, then: in some senses (yet in quite an illusory state), one is reborn.

What I also love about Sydney, or more particularly my area of Potts Point, is the number of people who are around day and night. No matter when I arrive, I know that when I walk towards the arterial route of Macleay Street there will be people moving back and forth. It reminds me of all those films I used to see as a child – films set in real cities like New York, where you could see, just behind the hero's shoulder, a street full of cars, with people hurrying off to mysterious destinations, to a lover or to jump off a building – or simply carrying home a meal which had been bought in a restaurant somewhere. All the bright immanence of city living seemed to cling to these people almost as if it were a phospherence, giving their most accidental trajectories all the beauty of a dance, a sense of people clustered together, yet living with a modicum of both civility and anonymity.

My jittery soul is soothed by Sydney, by its many voices, by the hundreds of faces which pour past me on the street, or sit facing me on a railway carriage – some tired, some radiant with a special beauty, some simply vacant as they read the horoscopes in a magazine, hoping to meet, or explore the alchemic possibilities which lie in chance.

Perhaps this is the secret of Sydney as a city to me – of all big cities. There is such an exponential increase in the possibilities of chance, of realising yourself, of meeting someone who is exactly like you, or unlike you, of greater varieties in ways of doing things. In that sense all cities are anagrams of chance, portraits of a complex self in restless resolution, ticking away with an insect intensity, forming and reforming, coming closer towards definition at the same time as everything round it stretches away into a landscape of seemingly infinite possibilities. I know it's partly an illusion, this sense of possibilities, of being reborn, of escaping, of becoming someone else – but the power of this illusion, its intoxication, is the secret charm of travel.

New Zealand is a small place and the sense of what is forbidden is ingrained into us and drops off like a discarded skin when you leave the country. It's almost impossible to say here how many and furious are the taboos which surround us on every side. In my youth these were sexual, or perhaps the sexual laws most affected me as a young homosexual. But these areas extend to your relationship to family, and your relationship to the culture itself.

As a Pakeha one grows up within the distortions of a post-colonial situation. I grew up in what was a quite naively materialist culture, stunted to a certain extent by various forms of trauma. The trauma of emigration is an act of division and removal from the mother land, a cutting off of links, or, as in New Zealand's case, an hallucinatory summoning-up of links to another part of the world – a world which isn't there.

I think this led to a kind of haunted being in New Zealand, which is best expressed in Janet Frame's works – the sense of dislocation, of other spiritual worlds existing, beating against the framework of the real like the wing of a wounded bird. And we live in a place of strong physicality where the spiritual voices from the indigenous culture have always been whispering in our ear, yet we trained ourselves over time not to be able to hear these truths.

This culture, Pakeha culture, has also been traumatised by repressed memories of its own native homelands. By my generation, the fifth to live in New Zealand, there are effectively no real connections to the place I belong to by racial background. Of course, this is not unusual. 'It is the fate of all migrants to be stripped of history,' says Salman Rushdie. Its effects, however, can be very real: I feel I grew up in what was in some senses a stunted culture. In Pakeha culture it is quite accepted that there is a huge and unbridgeable gulf between material culture and spiritual or artistic culture. Art is treated as some kind of optional gingerbread which can be placed on the house when the owner has enough money. It is not seen as the mode of expression, or way of seeing through problems. Artists in the widest sense, by which I mean architects, designers, thinkers and intellectuals, are not consulted to resolve problems: they are called in at the last moment to ornament economic brutalities.

We have moved, in my own lifetime, from a postwar society which had egalitarianism as its proudest boast into one which actively seeks to divide us into rich and poor, promoting these divisions in the belief that the trickle-down economy will enable a society that has been fragmented, atomised, deracinated and culturally impoverished somehow to continue to function adequately.

New Zealand is a very unhappy country. We are living through the butt-end of the failures of economic rationalism, in a society where the means of recognising or articulating this are limited. Isolation continues to be one of the strongest forces bearing on our culture: because we do not have enough information about what is happening in the rest of the world – because we have, by and large, inadequate newspapers and a television system in the English-speaking world – we continue to believe that our problems are unique rather than generic to post-colonialism, say. And we also fail to put our problems in a wider context.

Our country's unhappiness is compounded by a fundamental philosophical conundrum. The issues to do with the Treaty of Waitangi – that there are inalienable rights which must be honoured – cannot sit alongside economic rationalism, a fanatical faith that recognises no rights apart from those setting out to make profits. One ends up with a tacitly racist situation. The Treaty demands that some people, by their racial origin have rights which economic rationalism cannot touch. Other people by their racial origin have no special rights, even in the areas of their culture which have traditionally been the product of past excellence – for example, public health, the education system and even broadcasting.

If there was one reason I was happy to leave New Zealand it was to leave the sense of stalemate, of sourness, of unspoken things – things which it is now impossible to say. These taboos seem to dominate the country's discourse. Australia in many ways is no better. In some ways, racially it is much worse. But it's not my country. It can go to perdition and it isn't my problem. I'm here as an outsider – an interested outsider who likes this place but is not its citizen. I decided, as a New Zealand writer who had been politicised for several decades, that I would like to be disengaged for a while. It may seem cavalier but I thought perhaps this would give me a better perspective.

I also needed another kind of space. My primary relationship had been shot to bits and I needed somewhere that was distant but not too far away, to sit down and contemplate how much of me was left.

This is what Sydney is to me, then. A safe place. A neutral place. A beautiful foreign city in which they speak English and share some similarities. I like to live here as in a foreign land, because that's what this place is. Foreign. Other. Familiar. Different. As different as the birds which sound so stridently outside my window as the light dies down and the sense of a vast land mass permeates the air.

At the moment I live in both Auckland and Sydney. Both cities are dominated by harbours. I like to play, in mind's eye, with their differences. Auckland's harbour is shallow and tidal, dominated by skies which are constantly changing as winds blow in across the vast spaces of the Pacific. Sydney's harbour, by contrast, is deep, sequined, lapis blue, with skies by El Greco. The air is heavy with desert dust, with stage-scenery storms: all is vividness, drama – rock and brick. The city is like an encrustation, a low-level mollusc which has sprouted a defensive skin of mile after mile of tiled roofs, dour brick. There's a gravitas to Sydney despite its love of fireworks and sequins. Partly it's gravitational – it pulls people in – but it also has a physical weight, the heaviness of stone which you realise when they excavate and you look down into what is an enormous cube, as if they were carving blocks for some monstrous pyramid for the future: a putative city for a new race of giants.

Bravura – the outsized, the exaggerated – is the essence of Sydney's style. The Mardi Gras is a consummate expression of this. Sydney also has a well-developed sense of the frivolous. Each night, it seems, the skies fill with the pock of fireworks. The local citizens hardly bother to go to the windows to look. There has been an almost indefinite open season, it seems, of celebration of Australia as the 'lucky country'. Yet there's a sense of growing anticipation, too. Australia is on the point of wrenching off the British Crown and, with something of Napoleon's panache, crowning itself with a glittering Olympic diadem. There's a sense that world attention is about to beam onto this beautiful and, to some extent, unknown city. Perhaps there's also a slightly tender mood of these being last days – a lingering fondness for its rorty rooty laidback provincial beginnings. After all, there are not many cities in the world where it is so casually easy to live. There is also a feeling of apprehension about what the gross alchemy of international tourism might do – part of the pleasure of being here is the knowledge that not everybody in the world knows about it. Sydney has the delectable air of being, perhaps, the world's last best-kept secret.

You sense all these possibilities at Mardi Gras time, when the city goes en harlequinade. For one night a concentrated madness reigns. Yet it seems this spirit still informs the rest of the year – the lust for physical things, for sex, food, crime, intelligence, beauty of design. There's a want, even a wantoness in the city which is all about transformation, metamorphosis – propelling Sydney away from the provincial town it once was and turning it triumphantly, even ostentatiously, into that wonderful future state known as a world city.

Yet behind all the bravura, there's a ticking sense of nervousness too. Almost like a kind of vibration it stays there just at the point of furtherest audibility. It's a moot point how much more population this largely barren subcontinent can sustain. Overall, Australia is already one of the most highly urbanised societies on earth. There's also the further nightmare of Indonesia, the nearest neighbour with a population of over 200 million. It could easily collapse into civil war, unleashing endless fleets of boat people towards the apparently empty subcontinent to the south.

It's like Sydney salads: they're wonderfully artful, a mixture of Pacific and Eastern ingredients, but not everyone knows that the salad leaves, grown in local soil, are full of leached-out dioxins. The fact is that the soil round Sydney, after only 200 years, is effectively exhausted. It's overloaded with poisons. In this sense, Sydney seems to have the finite energy of a place like Hong Kong. It burns brightly, perhaps in part because its future is ambiguous. The almost yearly fires which ring

Sydney bring home this sensibility of doom and threat, of careless and vivid physical life, of living almost capriciously and purely for today. Friends have told me of the ashes fluttering down on Bondi beach during the days of bushfires. This apocalyptic vision seems to belong to Sydney too – somehow both a city of the future and a city of the past. In this sense, it seems a peculiarly ripe millennial city.

Yet there's a certain poignant moment I love above all in Sydney. It's that time in the evening when the light is turning towards night. The birds in the trees make sounds which tell me, again and again, I'm in a different country. The sounds are pensive, it seems to me, calling back into that vast interior which exists as a brooding presence – even in a city like this of over four million souls. There's a sadness, a clarity to these bird sounds: as if they had come out of some prehistoric moment and were calling both back into the past and into the future. Everything is so still. Inside lit rooms, people prepare their dinner. The sound of a shower patters up the lightwell. Moment by moment the magic of night closes in upon this vast subcontinent. And as if through some kind of hallucination, the birds lace over space and draw everyone back to some primordial moment, before cities existed – the dream time.

You can't escape, of course.

I was reminded of this the other day. There on the vestibule floor was a vast black woman, in stained jumpsuit. I'd seen her around the Cross in various doorways. She kept her belongings in plastic bags, and would keep up an endless ululating talk, a sort of one-person rap. I couldn't tell if it made sense, or was in some language I don't know. I don't even know if she's a Koori. But I do know she asked me in euphonious English for forty cents one day as I came out of the supermarket. I was so charmed I immediately gave it to her. I liked her manners. But this day was different. She had parked herself on the vestibule. She had lain down – beached.

When I came down the stairs there were two beldames from the apartment building. One was on a walker, and the other was similar: they're elderly relics from a more genteel period of Potts Point. They get their hair set each week; they swing off to do their tiny bits of shopping as made-up and carefully dressed as if they were going off to tea at Government House. One part of me admires their pluck. I'd like to think of myself at that age, being careful enough to dress well and bother with the reduced niceties of life.

Yet now the millennial world had arrived on their doorstep. The small Scots woman was bantering with the baglady, attacking her again and again like an angry terrier raised up on her hindlegs. 'You can't stay here,' she argued with plain enough logic. 'You have to move on,' cried the one with the walker-frame. Her hands gripped it as if she were seeking energy from its upright form.

'Where you from?' was the magnificent utterance of the baglady. Her voice was so orotund it might have been uttered by a major contralto. But there was such rage in her voice.

'Where you from?' She kept asking her unanswerable question to the Scots woman, who had perhaps lived most of her life in Australia but managed to keep the curlicues of her accent intact.

'Where you from?'

I thought – yes, there's no escape from the big questions of post-colonialism, or however you want to pose this endemic question. I could tell that the two elderly gentlewomen wanted me to take their side, simply because of the colour of my skin.

I was a cad. I walked off.

I don't live here, I thought.

And the next day the baglady was no longer there. She was sitting in another doorway, speaking that language which I couldn't understand and which might be nonsense, the psychobabble of the dispossessed, or it might be an explanation of how we all ended up here, just on the cusp of the millennium, in a city which is about to crown itself as one of the great cities of the next century – yet a city, too, in which people sleep on doorsteps, and kids plunge needles into their veins so they can dream of a better place.

It's all relative, I suppose. The fact is I'm truly happiest when I'm in neither city – or rather, when I'm up in the air, mid-Tasman. I like to look out the plane window at what is perhaps the ideal representation of

Peter Wells

space. In these moments the sharpness of perspective makes all problems seem soluble. Just beyond the wing tip, ahead, seems to lie the celestial city, the perfect city, the place where all is just right. Maybe one day I'll arrive there. Until then, I'll continue to live in both Sydney and Auckland. And in the words of Jan Morris, describing how she gets to know a place, I'll grin 'grin like a dog and run about the city'.

Journey to the Interior

Graeme Lay

'WE ... ANCHORED IN nine fathoms of water, within half a mile of the shore. The land appeared as uneven as a piece of crumpled paper, being divided irregularly into hills and valleys; but a beautiful verdure covered both, even to the tops of the highest peaks.' – Sydney Parkinson on the *Endeavour*, captained by James Cook, anchored in Matavai Bay, Tahiti, 13 April 1769.

Parkinson was a twenty-two-year-old artist from Edinburgh, a Quaker and a brilliant botanical illustrator. While the young artist busied himself drawing the myriad exotic plants of Tahiti, his shipmates fell under the spell of the island's women. The *Endeavour* was the third European ship to arrive at Tahiti, following the Englishman Samuel Wallis in *Dolphin* in 1767 and Frenchman Louis-Antoine de Bougainville in *Boudeuse* in 1768, so at the time Parkinson was writing the Tahitians were well aware of what the crews of the European sailing ships were seeking.

Cook's men must have thought they had arrived in Paradise, without the inconvenience of dying. The Tahitians had no inhibitions whatsoever about sex, and any constraints the Englishmen might have harboured quickly disappeared. The commonest price for sex was a nail, an exchange which was mutually satisfactory until the supply of nails dwindled and the very structure of *Endeavour* was endangered. But the happy swapping of steel for sex began a change in Tahitian society which has been compounded right through to today: the creation of an astonishingly mixed race of people.

Downtown Papeete, September 1997, 9am. Late-model Citroëns, Peugeots and Renaults are zipping along the four-lane waterfront carriageway, boulevard Pomare. Somewhere in the distance a klaxon wails. A smell of coffee, croissants, jasmine and tiare Tahiti – the fragrant national flower of Tahiti – is in the air. Tethered to the very doorstep of the town are luxury yachts from all over the Pacific, swaying gently in the harbour swell, their masts rocking like metronomes. On the pavements,

Journey to the Interior

people of all hues mingle and greet each other. *Bonjour. Bonjour. Ça va?* Many are families, the typical family consisting of a French father, a Tahitian, Chinese or mixed race mother and a pair of beautiful, caramel-coloured children. The 228-year-old love affair goes on.

Already the sun's heat is fierce, the sky high-gloss blue. Behind Papeete, rising steeply in ridges to verdant, jagged mountains whose peaks are wrapped in cloud, is the mysterious core of Tahiti, the 'crumpled paper' of Sydney Parkinson's journal. The mountains rise to well over two thousand metres, standing like green tusks guarding the heart of Tahiti. *La coeur de Tahiti*. It is a heart which I have never seen, but which I have long been curious about. What is in there? Lakes? Rivers? Valleys? Villages? Most visitors to Tahiti have a heart bypass, heading straight out to the other enticing islands of the Society group – Moorea, Huahine, Bora Bora. All I know is that in 1791 six of the mutineers from HMS *Bounty* fled up one of the valleys of Tahiti in an attempt to escape the vengeance of the pursuing Royal Navy, an expedition led by a hateful, heartless commander, Captain Edward Edwards of HMS *Pandora*. The six runaways made it into the interior of Tahiti, but the Tahitians, knowing full well on which side their breadfruit was buttered, betrayed the renegades. The mutineers were captured, returned to the coast and eventually to England to stand trial.

A four-wheel drive Toyota utility truck swings into the layby on boulevard Pomare. A tall brown man jumps out, shakes my hand, grins widely. 'Bonjour M'sieur. Je m'appelle Poken.' He hefts my case onto the back of the ute. His long hair hangs down his back; he wears a baseball cap, blue singlet, dark blue shorts. The circular patterned tattoos of the Marquesas Islands adorn his mahogany arms and legs.

As we swoop through the traffic of downtown Papeete and head out east of the town, Poken tells me that his mother is Marquesan, his father Tahitian. He honks and waves at people everywhere: gendarmes, road workers, taxi drivers. He explains that he is well-known through his cultural group performances. He plays guitar, ukelele and drums, has toured Europe, America, New Zealand. He also tells me proudly that he has two children: a boy of twelve called Teanuanua, which means rainbow, and a daughter of six called Orama, which means shooting star. Poken is also a cross-island guide, one of several who take people like myself into the interior of Tahiti. Now on the open road, we speed past Matavai Bay, where Cook anchored and Parkinson wrote of the mountain view, alongside the lagoon, shiny as shot silk in the morning sun, past outrigger canoes in which fishermen sit idly, past black-sand beaches, past surfers darting and twisting in glassy waves, and come to the village of Papeno'o. Poken swings the ute inland.

The valley of the Papeno'o river cuts wide and deep into the heart of Tahiti, I observe from the map on my knee. It is the dry season now, and the river runs gently through stones and boulders. The road beside it is unsealed, as rocky as the riverbed. To our right and left the sides of the valley rise abruptly to sharp, sinuous ridges hundreds of metres high, the bush extending from the valley floor to the skyline. From time to time we come across men operating earthmoving machinery on the banks of the river: front-end loaders, bulldozers, excavators. They are taming the river, making it tractable, digging trenches, laying culverts, building dams, steel bridges and small hydro-electric power stations which punctuate the river's flow. The Papeno'o is a source of power and fresh water for the people of coastal Tahiti: forty percent of the island's electricity comes from hydro-electric schemes.

Although in the wet season, from November to March, the in-spate river must be formidable, the going now is suprisingly easy. Poken's ute eases us over bumps and boulders, climbing steadily alongside the watercourse. Studying my map, I notice a recurring French word I have never seen before. *Gué.* There is a number beside it. Gué 1, Gué 2 and so on. 'What is gué?' I ask. Poken twists the wheel to avoid a boulder, frowns, tries to explain. 'It is when there is no bridge, but we still must cross. Go through the river in the truck.'

'Ah, a ford.'

Poken's frown deepens. 'No. Toyota.'

'No. Gué, a ford.'

'Toyota.' He points to the vehicle's name on the gear change. Before I'm able to explain, we come to a ford, a gué. Here the river is wide and swift. Poken drives straight into it. The truck becomes a kind of submarine as the water comes up to, then over the bonnet. The engine appears unaffected. As we emerge onto the shingle on the far side, I say to Poken, 'That was some gué. En Anglais, a *ford*.'

'Ah,' he says, understanding at last. But he is clearly struck by the irrationality of English. Why call a car after a place in the river that you drive through?

The river flows passively along its bed as we continue to climb alongside it. Opposite Gué 5 a waterfall, Cascade Vaiharuru, spills vertically to a pool, its backdrop a wall of bush-covered rock. We pass another hydro-electric station, a modern, tidy building set across the river. What strikes me is the absence of power lines or pylons. The fully automated stations have been designed by French engineers to blend with the valley environment. Transmission lines are all underground, so that apart from the small rectangular buildings and the low hum of the turbines within, the valley is undisturbed by the power developments.

Climbing more steeply now, we round a tight bend and pull over to the roadside for a fruit drink and a biscuit. Now I can see the head of the Papeno'o Valley. It is a vast basin eight kilometres in diameter enclosed by ramparts of rock and broken peaks, the remnants of a volcanic crater, a huge caldera which collapsed a million years ago. What strikes me is the scale and steepness of the mountains. On all sides there are walls of rock. The one which looks unclimbable is that which lies directly ahead, blocking the head of the valley like a massive fortress. This is Mount Tetufera, 1800 metres high and Tahiti's third-highest mountain. Tetufera is not a peak but a sheer wall, green like all the others but several kilometres across, its face grooved from top to bottom, cicatrices worn into the rock by falling water. Its summit ridge stands up dramatically against the blue sky.

'In the wet season,' says Poken, 'many cascades on Tetufera. Very beautiful.' It's not hard to imagine. The waterfalls must form a silver veil over the face of the mountain.

We pass another, larger dam, climb a zig-zagging metalled road and emerge onto a flat-topped ridge, on which is a complex of low buildings. Relais de la Maroto, the only inland hotel in Tahiti.

When the hydro-electric schemes began in the valleys of the island, a place was needed to accommodate the workers, to avoid the long, lumpy drive to Papeete and back every day. An accommodation block and dining area were built here, high up in the catchment zone. When the dams and powerhouses on the upper reaches of the Papeno'o River were completed, the hostel was converted to a hotel to accommodate those who wish to see Tahiti from the inside. *Relais* is one of those French words which is not quite translatable into English. It means a wayside inn with a reputation for fine food.

The directrice of Relais de la Maroto is a young Tahitian-born Frenchwoman, Christina Auroy, whose father built the complex for the workers. Poken goes off for a smoke with a mate and Christina shows me the the view from the deck. Only now do I realise that the *relais* is built right on the edge of a cliff. From the deck we look straight down to where the river tumbles through the bush and over basalt boulders, its course studded with pools of mountain-fed water. The only noise I can hear is gushing water. The air is still and scorching. Big dragon-flies like miniature helicopters hover about the deck railing. And talking of helicopters, out at the front of the hotel there is a helipad. For $150 you can take a trip up from Tahiti's Faa'a Airport in a helicopter, be whisked up and over the mountains, sweep up the valley and drop in for lunch at Maroto. That way you can also get to look *down* on Tahiti's highest peak, Mt Orohena, 2241 metres high and just over a ridge to the west of the Papeno'o Valley.

My room is on the top floor of the dormitory block. As I walk along the gallery past the other rooms I notice that they don't have numbers. Instead they have the names of French wines written on the door. 'Nuits Saint Georges', 'Château Lafite-Rothschild', 'Châteauneuf du Pape', and so on. I am shown into a room with 'Petrus' written on the door. This disappoints me. I've not heard of Petrus. I'd rather be in 'Château Lafite-Rothschild' next door – I know that's a fine wine. But 'Petrus' is clean, fresh and comfortable, and from the balcony there is an unimpeded view straight up the valley.

Noel, maître d'hôtel, Relais de la Maroto, and cellar-master.

Poken heads off in his truck, after agreeing to pick me up on his way through later in the week. After a siesta – the afternoon is still ferociously hot – I head up to the bar for a Hinano beer and there meet the maître d'hôtel, Noel. Like the majority of the people on the island today, he is part-Tahitian, part-French. Noel is an amiable young man, in spite of bearing what must be a considerable burden: his right hand and lower arm are heavily strapped and bandaged, the result of a fall in the mountains which gashed his wrist.

As we sit and talk I notice that of the men coming and going about the hotel, an unusual number are, like Noel, nursing injuries. Here a bandaged knee, there a strapped ankle, here a patched eye, there a dressed ear. The pharmaceutical industry in Tahiti must be booming. When these walking wounded meet, they greet each other with a handshake in the French manner, then refer to each other's injuries, proudly, as if comparing chest sizes. One man with a heavily bandaged leg limps up to Noel, grips his (left) hand, points to Noel's afflicted hand then at his own wound, and speculates as to which of them will be more handicapped sexually. Being French, neither concedes that there is a major problem. 'It's my hand that's strapped, not my dick,' Noel says to his friend with a laugh. As for this propensity to injury, a friend later explains that many Tahitians are reckless to the point of delinquency. They believe that they are immortal. Later, back in town, I witness this phenomenon. A family – two adults and two infants – crammed onto a Vespa, weaving through the rush-hour traffic; a girl on a bike, hanging onto the tray of a speeding truck; helmetless Vespa riders, racing three abreast down the motorway. *We are Tahitians, we are invincible.*

The Relais de la Maroto clearly remains a watering hole for everyone who still has work in the mountains. At lunch-times gangs of sweaty men, many wearing bandages, come trooping in for a beer and a meal, mixing readily with the well-dressed visitors who are passing through on a day excursion. As always in French-derived society, meal-times are sacred. The tables on the deck are filled with visitors: a melange of brown-skinned Tahitians, dusky New Caledonians, chic French, slender Chinese, and their offspring, children straight from the melting pot who will grow up without racial prejudice because they carry the genes of three regions: Europe, Asia and Polynesia.

One thing puzzles me about these visitors to Maroto, though.

When they arrive Noel takes them first not to the bar, not to the restaurant, not even to les toilettes. Instead they troop off with him down some steps beside Christina's office. When they return after about half an hour, they then go out to the deck to dine. After seeing this happen several times, I ask Noel where he takes the guests. 'Oh, à la cave,' he replies. 'La cave?' 'Ah oui. The cellar. Would you like to see it?'

We go down three flights of concrete steps to the bottom of the dormitory block. Noel unlocks a door, switches on a light and there it is – a long, cool room whose concrete, windowless walls are lined with partitioned wooden shelves, most of which are filled with bottles of wine. French wine. Very good French wine. At one end of the cellar there are tables and chairs, racks of glasses and, on the walls, maps of French wine districts, highly detailed maps colour coded with different vintages. Beaune, Côte du Rhône, Bordeaux. Noel explains that Christina's father, a wine-lover, came from the Beaune district of the Dordogne, one of France's best wine-growing regions. He brought his cellar with him, or rather he had one made, then shipped over 3000 bottles of French wine out to Tahiti and cellared them here in air-conditioned comfort,16 degrees Celsius. A wine club down in Papeete comes up here regularly for tastings. Casual visitors to Maroto also call in.

As I wander about savouring the coolness and the richness of the cellar, a thought occurs to me. 'Noel,' I ask, 'do you have a wine called Petrus?'

He makes a respectful face. 'Oh yes, we have three bottles of Petrus.' He takes me to a space where the trio of dusty bottles of red lie. 'They are our rarest wine.' He watches nervously as I pick up one of the bottles my room is named after. It has an unpretentious, even dowdy label. Later, when I study the Relais de la Maroto's wine list, I begin to appreciate Noel's nervousness. Petrus costs 93,900 Pacific French francs per bottle. In real money, that's $1192. I am happier with my room.

From the balcony of 'Petrus' I can see at the head of the valley an area of cleared, level land in the bush, on which there are some low rectangular structures. Consulting my map I work out that this must be the 'Site archéologique de Farehape Marae'. From boyhood I have harboured a fantasy of being an archeologist, so I grab my pack and head off down to the valley.

The road is rough and because of the steepness of the descent it doubles back on itself several times. At the bottom of the valley the heat is almost overpowering, and as I trudge along, awash with sweat, I curse myself for not bringing along a bottle of mineral water, a supplement that is de rigueur in the tropics. I feel as if I have been wrapped tightly in a hot wet blanket.

The road fords the river. The water flows swiftly here. To drink or not to drink? The water looks clean, but .... Aware that it takes only a teaspoonful of contaminated fluid to produce a violent reaction of the stomach, I pull back. I have made that mistake before. Parched, leaden-legged, I carry on up the road and a few minutes later come to the clearing.

The land is level and, although surrounded by dense bush, the coarse grass shows signs of having been recently attacked by a weedeater. I walk up onto the site of the ancient marae, a low platform of blackened, closely fitted river stones. In traditional Tahitian society the marae was the centre of community and ceremonial activities, an open-air space with vital social and religious functions. Here the primary gods Tane, Tu, Ro'o and Ta'aroa were worshipped, and here too a family's lineage was inscribed in stone, delineating its specific rank in society's hierarchy. The marae was also a memorial whose raised stones and posts recalled memories of deceased chiefs and ancestral lines. Here at Farehape, now that the bush has been cleared away, I can see that the several maraes are perfectly intact. The platforms of neatly fitting stones and the rectangular, low-walled enclosures with their several upright genealogical markers stand out starkly on the cleared land. A noticeboard informs me that some of the stone stages were archery platforms where the Tahitian elite carried out archery contests. Clearly, the Papeno'o Valley was once an area of vigorous social and religious activity. But why? And why did the people abandon such a significant settlement?

Then I notice at the far end of the terrace signs of human activity, a group of people doing some sort of work on one of the stone platforms. I stroll down to investigate. Most of the group are Tahitians, young people in shorts and singlets. Young men mainly, but also a couple of girls. They grin and greet me. 'Bonjour, M'sieur', 'Bonjour', 'Bonjour'.

A square about two metres by two metres and half-a-metre deep has been cut into the marae floor. Strings have been pegged across the small, neatly excavated quadrangle. In the background a bamboo platform has been set up. There are plans and notebooks on it. I would love to know exactly what is going on here, but how to ask? My French is not archeologically inclined. I observe that one man seems to be directing operations. He is a tall, athletic, deeply tanned, about thirty, a popa'a (a European) wearing a long, loose mauve singlet, shorts and a back-to-front baseball cap. I step up onto the marae and approach him.

'Ah, bonjour M'sieur. Je m'appelle Graeme. Je suis un écrivain de la Nouvelle Zélande. Q'est-ce que vous faites ici, s'il vous plait?' His tanned face breaks into a grin. He extends his hand. 'Hi. I'm Mark Eddowes, from New Zealand. I'm a PhD student at Otago University.'

Mark has been working in French Polynesia for eight years, excavating archeological sites from the Marquesas to the Australs. He has a traditional Tahitian tattoo on one leg, is fluent in Tahitian and French, and here in Papeno'o is supervising this group of young Tahitian archeology students. As we wander over the site he explains that this part of the Papeno'o Valley was once home to thousands of people, as were most of the valleys in Tahiti: 'There are hundreds of maraes throughout the interior of Tahiti. There's even one on top of the highest peak, Orohena.'

The fertile volcanic soil of the valleys supported crops of taro, sweet potatoes and bananas. The people lived in thatched fares built on stone foundations – paepae – surrounded by the marae, the focus of their religious and social activities. 'Tahitian society was strongly lithic,' Mark goes on. 'This was a source of stone for tools as well as building. We've been excavating the floors of various fares and we've found stone implements and the remnants of hearths. It was cooler up here at certain times of the year, so they needed fires for heating as well as cooking, and to keep mosquitos away probably.'

He also tells me that the inland valleys remained densely populated until the European missionaries arrived, from 1797 onwards. 'After the Tahitians were converted to Christianity the coastal areas became the centres of population. The people moved down to the coasts because the churches, mission schools and ports were built there. The interior of the island was largely abandoned after contact.'

Mark is an enthusiast, someone who has immersed himself in this reconstruction of Tahiti's traditional past. It's good to see the young people of Tahiti joining in, I suggest. He agrees. 'Most of them are very good students.' He pauses and shouts a directive to two lads erecting a shade tarpaulin over the excavation site. 'The main problem is stopping them smoking dope. Sometimes they go into the bush to cut a pole and they come back so stoned they forget what the pole was for.' Marijuana growing and smoking is rife in Tahiti.

On the way back, burning with the midday heat, I pause at a place where twin rivulets pour between boulders into a small deep pool. I strip off and slip into the mountain water. It is cool, clean, revitalising. Opening my eyes under water, I swim up to where it pours, foaming and bubbling, between the boulders. So fresh, so cool. It is like swimming in champagne. Vintage champagne.

In the evening I dine alone in the large, plush dining room. It is half dark and utterly silent, rather eerie. The young Tahitian waitress serves me the entrée, then vanishes. The serving is a minor work of art. It is a prawn terrine, smothered in a rich, brown Roquefort sauce. Its *pièce de résistance* is the front end of the shell of a small crayfish, presumably the former owner of the curved tail which crowns the terrine. The carapace is about three centimetres long, a beautifully smooth, rounded, ginger-brown shell. It has a long flat snout, a pair of very long, severally jointed front legs with elongated pincers, long thin whiskers and a cluster of secondary legs under its body. Its on-stalks eyes express astonishment at finding itself where it is. The whole, complicated arrangement of legs, eyes, feelers and claws remind me of a Swiss Army knife with all its bits and pieces extended. It is a freshwater crayfish, what the French call *une chevrette*.

When Noel comes into the dining room I express admiration for the creature's beauty and flavour. He tells me that the chevrettes live in the river and that Michel, one of the workers, caught this one last night. Then Noel has an idea. 'Would you like to go to catch some chevrettes tonight with the chef, Christian?' Certainly.

Michel, a huge Tahitian with a head like a cannon ball but with a gentle, considerate manner, lends me the pic – the many-barbed bamboo spear – he uses for the business. Last night, Michel says, he caught *beaucoup des chevrettes*, a whole bagful. The Maroto chef, Christian, lends me a torch and the pair of us head off down the steep, rocky road to the river.

Christian is about twenty-five. He comes from Strasbourg and likes living in the mountains because of the tranquillity and the outdoor life. 'No cars, no noise. The only sound here is the river.' At the bottom of the hill we come to the river. Although the moon is full and the sky is light, at ground level it is very dark. The riverbed is filled with the shadowy shapes of boulders and the sheen of moonlit pools.

Christian explains the technique. We shine our torches into the rock pools. When we spot a chevrette we hold the spear over him and still shining the torch, bring it down on his body, skewering him. It sounds very simple, and already I can see a large chevrette in a pool, his eyes turned fluorescent red by the torchlight. I hold the spear above him, aim, plunge it down on the chevrette. Supposedly. In fact my spear strikes only the stone over which the chevrette was lately hovering. Sweeping the pool with my torch, I can now see no sign of my quarry.

I move upstream, illuminate another pool, locate another chevrette. Shine, aim, strike, miss. Two-nil to the chevrettes. The problem is that the little crustaceans are very sharp-eyed and very quick. They dart, in reverse, at top speed in an instant. Then they vanish. I can see Christian's torch waving about downriver and hear him splashing about. I stumble over to the pool where he is hunting. He has just one chevrette in the bag. He suggests we try further downstream. Climbing over boulders, clutching our spears, we scrutinise every pool we come across. The large chevrettes seem to have vanished completely. Now there are only tiny ones who drift about, waving their antennae lazily. After an hour, hot, tired, wet and frustrated, we give up.

Taking the long, steep road back up to the relais, Christian observes, 'The Tahitians say that when the moon is full, it is no good for catching the chevrette.' The empty-handed fisherman's oldest defence – blame the moon. We look up reproachfully at the gleaming globe. Then I think of those scarpering mutineers from the *Bounty*, the ones who ran away up here from their pursuers. Now I realise it was a good thing that they did get caught. If they hadn't, they would have gone mad trying to catch chevrettes.

I'm having lunch on the deck on my last day when a big hand descends on my shoulder and another one is extended in greeting. It is Poken, come to collect me and take me down the mountain. We climb into the Toyota and head off in the direction of Tetufera.

Now the road is not really a road, it is just a grassy track, barely three metres wide, winding torturously around bluffs and ridges. To our left is a ravine hundreds of metres deep; ahead is the great green face of Tetufera, so sheer and high that it is obvious that no road could conquer it. How will we get over it? I don't ask Poken. He is concentrating on keeping the truck on the track, wrestling with the wheel and the gear lever, face set grimly. Some corners are so tight that we can hardly get around them. The road is still climbing, and although the long grass on it suggests that it is not often used, I cannot imagine what would happen if we met another vehicle coming the other way. One of us, I suppose, would have to reverse. That thought makes my palms greasy.

Now the narrow road is climbing along the face of the mountain, past waterfalls and bush-covered bluffs, still with the dizzying drop to our left. I can manage a moment of admiration for whoever it was who incised this road into the cliff, but I'm still bothered by where it will all end. We're now well over 1500 metres high and still climbing. Then, lo and behold, the road swings hard right. A tunnel, cut straight through the volcanic rock, grids of reinforcing steel plastered into its roof and sides. Water pours from the roof of the tunnel, which is about a hundred metres long. We slosh through and out the other side. 'Very good toonell,' says Poken, and I have to agree. French engineering must be on a par with French cuisine.

On the other side of Tetufera it is all downhill and perilously steep. On several hairpin bends Poken has to reverse and have two shots at cornering. This backside of the mountain is clearly wetter, and we pass through rainclouds and stands of tropical rainforest, huge trees whose boughs and foliage enclose the road. Cataracts spill down the rampart of rock to our left, draining away down the mountainside to Lake Vaihiria, Tahiti's largest natural lake.

Gradually, carefully, we follow the river course down the ravine, driving through the mountain mist and rainforest to the lower reaches of the valley, still enclosed on all sides by vertical walls of rock.

Barrages, man-made lakes and small power stations appear again. Far ahead I can see a patch of blue sky. At last the road levels out as the valley floor widens. There is a house, some coconut and banana palms, plots of taro. Minutes later, more buildings, an expanse of greenhouses, then the valley opens out and merges with the coastal plain in the commune of Mataiea, once home for a time to Paul Gauguin and Rupert Brooke. The sky is clear and blue, the lagoon sparkling under the afternoon sun.

Tahiti's interior has been penetrated, its heart explored. As I look back at those huge, green, soaring mountains, I think again of awestruck Sydney Parkinson's description: *'as uneven as a piece of crumpled paper ... a beautiful verdure ... even to the highest peaks'.* Poor Parkinson – the brilliant artist was never to see England again. He contracted dysentery in Batavia and died on the Indian Ocean in January 1771. But his marvellous botanical illustrations of Tahiti endure, as does his description of the island, a peerless summation of the everlasting allure of a high tropical Pacific island. Time, one might say, expands in order to visit the number of high Pacific Islands in existence. Parkinson's Law.

Then there is Moorea. Not only explorers and artists but also writers, scientists, and sundry scapegraces from all over have been entranced by the sight of *that* high volcanic island, Tahiti's near neighbour. It is the first thing that visitors to Papeete notice, and one of the last things they see as they leave. Moorea is just eight minutes away by light plane from Tahiti; twenty minutes by catamaran, forty by car ferry. Any way you go it's a treat. From the air you can stare down on Moorea's multiple Matterhorn peaks, the mottled pink of its lagoon, the white ruffle of its reef waves. The approach by sea causes the island's green spires to seem to rise up from the water so that their features come slowly and hypnotically into focus.

But to appreciate Moorea it's not even necessary to go there. It's enough to watch its shifting moods from Papeete. Early in the morning the island's peaks are are a soft, gin-and-tonic blue. By day they are usually concealed by a mosquito net of gauzy cloud. In the late afternoon the clouds lift and the sinking sun backlights the island, bringing the mountains into sharp, silhouetted relief. But it is in the early evening, when the Earth has rotated a few more degrees, that Moorea and the sky turn on their best show.

Back in my waterfront hotel after traversing Tahiti, I am again mesmerised by Moorea, as no doubt Sydney Parkinson was too, as he strolled along the black sand of Matavai Bay. My hotel is not in the prettiest part of Papeete: it's at the end of Boulevard Pomare – the part the locals call the Gaza Strip – right across from the Quai de Moorea. By night the streets are full of strutting matelots and strident music. Raucous vehicles roar past the plump Tahitian hookers who lurk in the shadows of the bars' colonnades.

My hotel is, to put it gently, unpretentious. Its small vestibule contains a few vinyl armchairs, some soft-drink and cigarette vending machines and a TV set which is never turned off. The receptionist is a kind Tahitian girl who gives me a fruit drink every time I change my New Zealand dollars for Polynesian francs because she pities the exchange rate. Through the tatty curtain behind her, always smoking, sits a morose, aging Chinese man with a face as pale as the rind of uncooked pork. The whole building has a sad, soiled, profitless feel about it. I suspect that some of its rooms rent by the hour, judging by the frequency that different couples come and go through the vestibule and up the clunky lift that carries them to its higher floors. Another curious feature of the hotel is that is has no restaurant or dining room. Finding a place to eat is no problem, however, as every evening across on the waterfront dozens of little food vans – called here *les roulottes* – trundle up to dispense eveything from crepes to kebabs. Their braziers glow in the hot black night and the aroma of their dishes hovers about the quai.

On my second-to-last night in Papeete I sit at a roulotte and look up from my plate of crêpes suzette. It is then that I notice that my hotel is very high, a fact that I had not previously realised, my room being on only the second floor. Now I can see that from the top floor of the hotel there would be a grand view of the waterfront and of Moorea, a panorama which I long to capture on film.

The next day the sky is almost totally clear, suggesting that sunset conditions will also be favourable. At six o'clock that evening I take the jerking lift and my camera to the fourteenth floor of the hotel. Outside the lift is a small, gloomy landing and a set of bare concrete stairs. At the top of the landing is another landing covered with dusty, stacked tables and chairs. Behind the stack is a solid door bearing the notice 'Restaurant Capitaine Cook'. I push past the furniture and try the door. Locked. *Merde!* In minutes the sunset will be starting, and there is no window, no balcony, no view and, thus, no photo. Then I notice another stairway, to the right of the landing. At the top is another door. Knowing that it too will be locked, I perversely climb the stairs and try the door handle. It turns, the door opens.

Before me is a wide, slightly convex expanse of asphalt. There is a concrete shed and a big TV antennae beside the door, but the roof is otherwise bare. I walk across to its leading edge. It is like standing on the brink of a canyon. There is no guard rail, no guttering, just an updraft of tropical air. Far, far below is Boulevard Pomare, its vehicles as tiny and silent as cars on an architect's model. To my left and right, already pricked by firefly lights, are the buildings of Papeete. Behind them are Parkinson's serrated mountains, now darkened and looming. But my eyes do not linger on those mountains, the town or the boulevard below. Instead I stare ahead, over the waterfront, over the channel, at the jagged line-graph profile of Moorea.

There are only smudges of cloud in the western sky. As the sun slips below the horizon the sky flares, suffusing the entire horizon with light, saturating it with colour. Red, orange, vermilion. And beneath the sky, looming like a black iceberg, is Moorea. The scene is operatic and I am in the royal box. I feel like the Queen of Tahiti.

With startling speed the colours begin to fade, as if a dimmer switch is being turned somewhere in the mountains behind me. I pick up my camera, frame the scene, pause, press the shutter.

Moorea from the top of Papeete.

A London Engagement

Barbara Else

A Passion for Travel

IN JUNE 1997 Macmillan UK wrote and asked if I'd be prepared to fly over for a promotional tour of England, Scotland and possibly Ireland when they published my first novel in Britain. I don't like travel. I don't particularly like reading travel books. I don't even like reading the reviews of travel books. I did not want to go.

But from my work as a literary agent, let alone life as a writer, I know how hard it is to get new authors noticed: difficult enough in their own country, far more difficult abroad. *The Warrior Queen* had done well in New Zealand but there could be no guarantee it would do the same elsewhere. Here was a large international publishing company prepared to promote the novel vigorously. They were also in the process of buying my second novel, *Gingerbread Husbands*. I began to realise that my answer should probably be yes. Like most introverts in such circumstances I said, 'I'll think about it,' and pretended that it just would never happen.

It couldn't be certain that my being on the spot in Britain would help sales anyway. The best my local publisher, Brian Phillips of Godwit, could say was, 'It can't hurt. At the least it will make an impression on the trade, and that's important.'

Being away from home would mean no obvious or direct earnings for me during that period. It might be a lot of hard work with no gain: some loss, in fact as Macmillan could not pay all expenses, which would mean flying economy class – invariably cramped, tedious, and smellier as the hours pass. I experienced extremes of fear and loathing. What if I had to sit next to a loud-mouthed extrovert? What if I had to sit next to a hugely fat person who hogged the armrest, or someone with a well-developed head cold?

Over the next weeks I learned a little more about Macmillan's plan. They wanted to promote four new writers at once, in February 1998. They would call it the Fab Fiction Tour, and us the Fab Four, which provided my first laugh. The other authors were two young English women with their first novels, Harriet Castor (*Firebird*) and Gay Longworth (*Bimba*), and an established Australian writer, Nick Earls

(*Zigzag Street*). We would travel around doing readings and book signings.

The media in New Zealand picked up on the Fab Four tour when *Gingerbread Husbands* was published here. One editor phoned me. 'There's a second news story in the tour,' he said. 'I don't think so,' I said. 'Yes!' he cried. So to my embarrassment I saw a headline 'Kiwi Writer gets British Accolade'. Some people thought I'd won a prize. Now I'd really have to go – that's if it ever happened. The alternative would be to hide in my wardrobe for a fortnight and make up stories about how successful and exciting it all was.

The best-laid plans of all publishers' publicity departments can meet with impassable indifference from newspaper editors, radio producers, and bookshops. From the first I doubted there would be a tour to Ireland. As weeks went by the itinerary definitely rendered down. London, Manchester and Edinburgh became London, Manchester and Bradford (Bradford?), then London and Manchester. From two weeks, the tour condensed to ten days, then one week. Co-ordinating four writers was obviously not simple for Macmillan, though from my point of view it all began to seem more manageable. But I did not want to leave my husband Chris. I did not want to leave my home and perfect summer garden, nor my elderly cat Alcatraz, who pined whenever I was away.

Time came when I had to book my tickets: directly there and back, two days in London before the tour to get over jet-lag, one extra day at the end. I also took insurance against the whole thing being cancelled. Perhaps I'd go, but nothing would be organised – see impassable indifference, above – and I'd sit in my hotel room biting my thumb for a week. At least my older daughter Emma was in London, and I'd be able to see her.

With three weeks to go, an initial PR schedule was emailed from Macmillan, and it began to look as if it would be a reasonably busy tour after all. But February, in London and Manchester. Winter. Oh dear God, I had just gone through my wardrobe and tossed out nearly all my winter clothes. I faxed Emma, asking what elegant middle-aged women in the publishing/literary world were wearing over there. 'Bring a warm coat,' she faxed back. 'Bring a warm scarf and gloves. You will need a hat.' I loathe and detest hats. I would not take a hat.

The horror of travel still lurked behind each breath I took. I thought of the intrepid Victorian women who managed deepest Africa and decided that getting organised might help. I stocked up on little medical essentials to keep me going in front of interviewers and audiences: Vitamin B for stress, 'bee-juice' lozenges for speaker's throat, Vitamin C and garlic pearls to ward off colds. I bought a travel alarm clock, a travel iron – if I was to appear in front of audiences, I ought to be uncrumpled. I bought a folding umbrella: green with yellow cats on, very cheering. I had a hair cut. I had a facial. I visited my dentist. 'If the promotion fails,' he said after the de-plaquing, 'it won't be because of your teeth.'

I realised too that I'd better read *The Warrior Queen* again and clarify what I would need to say about it. This isn't as easy as it sounds – I was two books on from it by that stage and was deep into the writing of another.

Being sensible about it, of course I knew I had to go on this trip because it is simply part of the business of being a writer. I had also had experience here at home, reading my work to audiences, being interviewed. Surely it wouldn't be too different, over there? But while I was feeling a little more able to go and do the job, I was also feeling small and insignificant. This was my big chance. What if I blew it? If so, I would have let down my local publisher who had made a contribution to the travel costs, Chris, my daughters and other family. Also, each little overseas success by a New Zealand writer means it becomes easier for others to get published there – I really had better not blow it. Fear, loathing and now increasing terror – especially when Brian phoned with comforting advice: 'By the time you get back, more people will have heard of you than twenty times the population of New Zealand. None of them might read books, mind you,' he added. Brian knows that to make me laugh is the right way to get me to do things.

Then, two days before I left, a fax came through for me: an invitation to speak at the Vancouver International Writers Festival in October 1998. I was completely astonished but, oddly, it also helped to steady me. It was an affirmation that I had some international literary recognition – I didn't have to understand why – and that I would have other chances, even later on this year.

It was terrible saying goodbye to Chris at the airport. I would have to be without him on this, the biggest professional engagement of my life. Yes, I could do it. But I truly did not want to.

'Pacific' Class (oh dear, we really are not stupid) on Air New Zealand was not as bad as I had feared: it was superlatively worse. 'New ergonomically designed seating,' boasted the in-flight magazine. When I read it, half an hour after getting on the plane, I already had discomfort in parts of my musculature that usually feel pretty good. It was certainly different from the old seating, in that it tortured you in another position. I sincerely, deeply hope that any Air New Zealand board member or senior executive who sins against company rules is buckled into a Pacific Class seat and left there for a minimum of ten hours.

I was to be met at Heathrow by a taxi ordered by Macmillan, and by my daughter who would get there by tube and drive back to the hotel with me. When I emerged jet-lagged and bleary from the Customs hall I saw an imposingly large man holding a sign with 'Mrs Barbara' printed on it. As I began to ask if he might mean Barbara Else, Emma materialised in front of me saying, 'I thought that could be you, and it is! Hi, Mum!' The driver gruffly and efficiently established which hotel I was booked into, agreed I was the right Mrs Barbara and whizzed off with my trolley. Emma strode after him. I clung to her and managed to keep up.

Driving in to London, and checking into the small but perfectly formed hotel in Pimlico chosen by Macmillan because it was close to their offices, I began to feel excited at last. I really was a writer at the start of a promotional tour. People had expected me; there was a room booked; a bouquet of yellow tulips and giant hyacinths arrived from my editor at Macmillan.

From the window of my tiny squeaky-clean room, London was mostly grey: dirty pewter sky, rows of grey Mary Poppins chimney pots, grey walls – but on a grey roof directly opposite, the most glorious bright patch of emerald green. Moss. My tired eyes appreciated it immensely, but I was glad I didn't live beneath it.

Emma helped me figure how to work the plumbing so I could have a shower – a state of jet-lag is not conducive for nutting out new shower systems – and we decided to walk and find a place for lunch. I'd been travelling for thirty or so hours, and had to stay awake another six at least.

It was marvellous, walking with my tall, beautiful, intelligent daughter, both of us in long black coats and boots, both of us writers. My excitement battled with the jet-lag. 'I'm amazed that I am flavour of the month,' I said to Emma,' 'when I only ever expected to be the drip at the bottom of the cornet.' 'Did you make that up?' she asked with pleasing admiration. Otherwise, most of my sentences seemed to hit brick walls in the middle and both ends ended up lost. As the light began to fade late afternoon, I decided I would let myself fade too, and try for another day tomorrow.

Less jet-lagged on the Saturday, I bought a hat. I also looked at the latest copy of my individual publicity schedule. I would meet my editor and the PR team on the Monday. About twenty interviews had been organised for me, mostly for radio, the bulk of them to be done at Broadcasting House in Portland Place, a step away from Oxford Street. I would have a minder with me all the time. I was to give a talk at the Institute of Commonwealth Studies, and the Fab Four together would do some readings and travel to Manchester. A launch party was planned for the end of the week.

It was the first major item on the schedule that gave me the most trouble: taxi to Abbey Road for photo shoot. No, I thought, they wouldn't. They can't mean it. That is totally over the top.

I met Nick Earls on the Sunday night. He and I had a drink in the bar of our hotel and found we had a lot in common. We'd enjoyed each other's books, were very interested in the craft of narrative, in good storytelling techniques. Nick's *Zigzag Street* with its strong central character, a young partnerless male searching for love and a good diet, is gently sardonic, enlightening about men and very funny. We discussed the fact that Macmillan were not promoting us as Australasian writers, just as new writers, and also the different qualities of the Fab Four novels. Clearly, the promotion was angled to catch four different sections of the market and there would not be any rivalry between us.

That seemed true even at our first meeting as a foursome on the Monday. I found the two young women increasingly interesting as the week went on. Harriet had published children's books since the age of twelve but *Firebird*, a romantic novel was her first for adults and she was particularly nervous at our first reading. Gay, a former 'It-Girl', was loaded with confidence. I heard her novel, *Bimba*, described as a kind of female *Trainspotting*.

Macmillan did mean it about the photo shoot on Abbey Road. We went by taxi to the famous Beatle crossing outside the Abbey Road recording studios. The police had said we could go ahead with it. They'd also said that they took no responsibility for any drivers we held up becoming violently bad-tempered. But it was fun, although I was (alphabetically) selected to be first. I felt very burdened: if I didn't scoot out of the way of traffic quickly enough, the three behind me might be smooshed just as the week began. We tried again and again to get our feet on the right stripes and stand there without wobbling. The photographer was very brave, I thought, snapping away with her back to the oncoming lorries. Most drivers grinned. Nick Earls swears that George Harrison drove past in a nifty sportscar and waved to us.

Macmillan's 'Fab Four': Barbara Else (John Lennon) followed by Gay Longworth (Ringo Starr), Harriet Castor (Paul McCartney) and Nick Earls (George Harrison). We all wanted to be the enigmatic George.

My first solo engagement was the talk at ICS. I was nervous, but not as much as later on. Emma was chairing the session, and I knew some of the audience had already read *The Warrior Queen*. I grabbed this chance to acknowledge New Zealand women writers whose example and encouragement have been and still are important to me. The occasion was made very lively by Gina, my minder for the day, who has a fund of gossipy publishing stories and carried with her everywhere during the week an animal-like floppy fur hat. My favourite Gina story was about Jackie Collins being terribly upset that her latest novel would be advertised on posters in the London Underground. She was afraid nobody would see them.

The first joint Fab Four reading was at Waterstone's Bookshop in

Islington. Audience numbers were good – something that can never be predicted, especially at a launch of new writers. We'd decided on a reading order. Harriet went first because hers was the most serious book. I followed with two short excerpts from my funny one, Gay did her piece and we ended with Nick. I'd been worried that my selection, which went down well at home, might not suit an English audience. Laughs came at exactly the same places and I sat down with my pulse thudding.

The first night Gay chose a piece where one of her characters was beaten up and urinated on. The distaste on the faces of the audience must have spoken to the Macmillan people there, for next night at Ottaker's Bookshop in Clapham, Gay told the audience that she had been asked not to read that excerpt again. She described exactly why not, then read a piece where a character vomited inside a car. On the third night, she went back to her first piece.

Harriet chose new pieces for the second reading as well, having realised how to use an audience. I really enjoyed seeing her confidence grow during the week. It was exciting to learn she'd been given one of the WH Smith Fresh Talent awards for *Firebird*.

We stayed with the reading order each night, and Nick and I also stayed with the pieces that we'd found worked with audiences at home and worked in Britain too. Nick is an experienced and fluent performer who told us that he began his literary career as a story-telling armchair at the Brisbane Writers Festival.

Audience numbers at each bookshop continued to be good, and they were such wonderful bookshops – it was a week of torment, going into these full, well organised shops and not having the chance to look around properly. We had interviews there, did signings and the readings, then had to answer questions from the audiences and rush off.

The trip to Manchester was not necessarily a highlight but I wouldn't have missed it for anything. Four Macmillan editors came with us on the minibus, a four-hour-plus trip on the grey M6 under the horizonless pewter sky of winter England. We stopped for a late lunch at a Welcome Break, one of those alienating, surreal highway rest-spots in the middle of nowhere where you have a choice of soggy hot food or rigor-mortised sandwiches. As dusk fell, we drove past Grenada Studios. The street outside was lined with star-shaped portraits of Coronation Street characters, outlined in yellow lights.

We straggled into Waterstone's Deansgate for our reading. The bookshop had another session on as well that night – Robert Temple, whose book *The Sirius Mystery* explains how earth has been visited by educators from another galaxy. He was on the upper storey, very suitable. We were on ground level.

Our reading went better than ever that night. I was even more frustrated at not being able to look around this shop. It was like something from a modern Dickens – chaos, colour, and a slew of computers in the underground warren of the staffrooms. As we left, the Deansgate staff seemed bouncing with the fun of it: it was the biggest turnout they'd ever had for new writers. Then the Macmillan PR team told us that it was crucial for new books to 'knock over' this bookshop. If Waterstone's Deansgate thought you were okay, the rest of the regional bookshops seemed to follow. We piled back into the minibus (the driver had grown very grumpy) and stopped at the same Welcome Break as on the way up. Real déjà vu at 11 pm is far too much like jet-lag.

During the week I was tickled to see that people in UK publishing actually do greet each other and say goodbye with *mwah-mwah* kisses. Back in London that night as we gradually dropped off the others from the minibus, everyone was giving and receiving little kisses. Nick and I were to be last out of the van. I knew what he was thinking, precisely what was in my own head: *when in Rome? No thanks.* At the elevator door, on the second floor of the Holiday Inn Express Hotel, Belgrave Road at 1 am, we wished each other a good night's sleep and good interviews next day, and staggered off, un-mwahed.

On tours like this, the authors feel like – and should be – performing seals, put in the right place at the right time by their minders, the PR people. It's your job to do as well as you possibly can, focus on your book, haul interviewers back to the topic if they try to shuffle away, then shut up and be carted along to the next event or interview, and keep your energy levels high. Sophie, my minder during my solid days of interviews, was brilliant. I spoke to radio stations all over Britain: some interviews were live, some were recorded for arts programmes later on. With bright intelligent charm and efficiency Sophie ferried me to Broadcasting House and other independent radio stations, sat with me during each session, made sure I got everywhere on time. She was getting over a bad back so I encouraged her to lie on the floor of the tiny studio booths at Broadcasting House – just room for her, me, a desk, a microphone – while I did my stuff with whatever voice was on the other end of the line in whatever part of the country.

Sophie gave each interviewer points out of ten, something I found very comforting somehow, especially seeing her hand rise up above the desk top from her prone position on the floor. She scored BBC Radio Scotland eight-and-a-half out of ten: they had me discussing the opening of Salman Rushdie's first, unheralded novel *Grimus* with the head of the Arvon Foundation, a Scottish writing school. They had also organised a reading from *The Warrior Queen* to begin the session. It is a shock to hear your own dialogue suddenly coming at you in strange English voices.

BBC Radio Suffolk got five out of ten: I was wedged in an afternoon community round-up session, after waffly chatter about taking rum and cloves to cure your cold and a request from the local repertory theatre for a luminous stuffed donkey.

My highlight for the trip was an interview with Anna Raeburn for Talk Radio. It came towards the end of a hectic day. Sophie saw I was beginning to flag. When Anna came hands outstretched to meet me, saying she wanted to do a full half-hour because she loved the book so much, I thought, *I have no energy.* Anna went to sort out the studio, and I asked Sophie if she could phone my UK literary agent to delay the appointment I'd set up with her. Sophie had it done in half a minute while I caught my breath. Astonishing, and very uplifting. My energy levels surged. Having a PR person do the tiniest thing for me, without any hesitation, was a sign that I really had made it. Sophie gave Anna eleven out of ten.

It was a week of total focus such as I'd never had before. I did not dare relax. Each day Chris phoned but I was longing to get home and unwind with him, sitting in the sunshine in our fernery. 'When I get back,' I said, 'I don't know whether I'll burst into tears or just start talking.' 'You're welcome to do both at once,' he said.

Travel writing is meant to be packed with visual detail – one night, from a taxi, on a road verge somewhere near Buckingham Palace I saw a row of gently nodding red cordylines. They were disorientating, so familiar but so far from home. I saw the shabby carpet in the corridor of Broadcasting House, the mysterious doors along its walls which Sophie said she'd never seen anyone go into. I saw the water cooler, other people swotting up their notes before their interviews. I saw the pewter sky. When I'd visited London eighteen months before, Chris and I had travelled on the Underground most of the time and popped up from stations like a pair of groundhogs to peer around and get our bearings. This time, with Macmillan paying for taxis, I appreciated the upper surface of London, how the Thames curves, how romantic the bridges are when they're lit up at night.

There were some funny moments. After one bookshop event a tall City gent with a briefcase, in a pinstriped suit with a billow of white silk handkerchief in his breast pocket, came up to Nick and me. 'I've never been able to tell the difference between an Australian and New Zealand accent,' he said. 'Listening to you people tonight, I still can't hear a difference. Is there one?' 'There uzz,' I said. 'There ees,' said Nick.

A London Engagement

The City gent looked disbelieving as he strolled off. 'Barking mad,' muttered Gay who was standing at our shoulders. We glanced at her, in surprise, and saw the likeness. Daughter and dad.

The last radio interview was the only one where I didn't have a minder. I had told Sophie that she must keep a doctor's appointment for her back, that I could manage on my own by now. The scheduled host had been changed from a woman who'd read and liked my book to a young man who was an author himself and seemed trying to score his own points. And this was a live broadcast, on Greater London Radio. Afterwards I climbed into my taxi and told it to go to Emma's. She rushed out saying, 'I heard it, you were great!'

'That was the worst interview I have ever done,' I told her. 'Let me give you a cup of tea,' said Emma, 'then you can listen. I taped it.'

The cup of tea was wonderful. I suppose the interview wasn't as bad as I had thought: at one point, I did call the interviewer a clever boy.

On my last day in London, the publicity all done, I walked to the Tate Gallery to meet Emma. The weather had been warm all week. Cherry trees had started to blossom; the first spears of spring bulbs were showing. I'd worn the new hat only twice. Halfway to the Tate I found a tiny park near Bessborough Street and sat with the unseasonable sunshine on my face, listening to the fountain and shaking with quiet happiness. The tour was over. I had done it. And I'd done it as well as I could.

That afternoon, Emma and I went into one of my favourite bookshops in the world, Silver Moon in Charing Cross Road. Right inside the door at eye level was a stack of *The Warrior Queen*. I went out again very quickly.

Travel home was – well, I did that, too. An air hostess chatting with the men in the row in front of me said, 'It's so hard to unwind after one of these trips, you've had four hundred people in your face for over twelve hours.' Great PR, wouldn't you say? She should have had some lessons from Macmillan. One thing I learned from her, though: if you tell a hostess that because of the appalling seats you're in extreme skeletal and muscular pain, she'll bring you a packet of pain-killers.

After the thirty hours' travelling, I still didn't know what I'd do when I saw Chris for the first time. Who knew, at that stage, if the trip had been successful? I might not know for six months or more. But even at that stage, I knew I'd go again. Stressful, definitely; nerve-wracking, exciting and intense – and I had relished every minute.

As I walked down the passenger corridor at Wellington Airport and saw Chris waiting right in front of the automatic doors I broke into the widest grin I've grinned in all my life.

Safeguarding *the* Cotton Castles

Tessa Duder

SOMETHING TERRIBLE BUT necessary happened at a small tourist resort called Pamukkale in south-western Turkey in mid-1997. An edict, fences, signs, with a concerned world's weight behind them, stopped two million people in their eager tracks. Approaching the third millennium, no longer are ordinary people able to experience directly through the soles of their own mortal feet one of the world's great natural wonders. From now on, in the name of protecting for all time the geological curiosity that has attracted travellers since Greek and Roman antiquity, it's strictly feet off, hands off, people off.

A terrible deprivation, says part of me, but inevitable and necessary and about time, says another part.

Early in 1997, visiting my daughter and her Turkish family and unaware of my personal good timing, I must have been one of the last few hundred ordinary folk to walk and climb extensively and at awestruck leisure over the famous white travertine terraces at Pamukkale. In March there was still snow in the air, a biting wind, and an early spring haze over the plains of the river Meander and its tributary, the Lucos. To the south, snow still lay on the mountain range between Denizli and the Aegean coast some two hundred or more kilometres away. It's not high season, when all most tourists want to do is swim and sunbathe, but it's good weather for walking.

To reach the crest rising steeply about one hundred and fifty metres above the village, along with the famous hot pools and the ruins of the city of Hierapolis, I could have caught a local bus up the new ecologically-driven road that now meanders (yes, the word derives from the river) up and around six kilometres of adjacent barren hillside; I could have taken the direct road curving up one flank of the terraces that, until it was closed about seven years ago, was used by locals and tourists to drive up to the crest. I chose instead to walk up one of the narrow ridges that define the outer boundaries of the great main amphitheatre of iceberg-white travertine. That way, I was told by my canny son-in-law who owns a carpet shop in the village, I would avoid having to pay an entrance fee and would most appreciate the terraces' sheer size, their astonishing and delicate beauty. There was only one restriction: on the terraces, no shoes. I wasn't, and didn't feel like, an ordinary tourist who comes in by air-conditioned tour bus from Izmir, Denizli, Ephesus, Istanbul, Ankara or Antalya, and stays for half a day, overnight at most. I was an honorary local walking as locals did, with a Turkish family and nearly two weeks to explore the terraces at my own time.

The path begins as a narrow stone wall above a field of cotton and rises steeply as a slim rocky rib, less than a metre wide in places, turning white about a third of the way up where the calcium-rich spring water has reached and left its deposit over many centuries. Put a frame around the scene coming into close focus, and you'd swear you were on a snowfield. White crusts lie thickly on trees, icicles up to three metres long hang down from staircases of scalloped cups. Aren't those regular rounded bumps *moguls*, those smooth slopes areas of *piste*? The illusion of snow begun as you first saw the distant white scar on the hillside approaching from Denizli twenty kilometres away, and now even more in close-up, is complete.

Except for what you are now feeling with your bare feet. Even in early spring the surface holds a little residual warmth. It's certainly not cold enough to turn your toes blue; neither is it sharp-edged, stony or slippery. It's like walking on smooth white matte pottery – I was put in mind of the serene white works of Auckland potter John Parker – and extraordinarily benign on the soles of tender, normally-shod human feet. When I first realised that I didn't have to worry about slipping over, nor getting cut about the feet even on the sharpest-looking ridges, I relaxed.

Nearing the top, the famous shell-shaped pools of a million tourist posters and postcards are now close by. They comprise a relatively small proportion of the whole, and they are more whimsical, more magical, more extraordinary and bizarre than anything Walt Disney or Antonio Gaudi could ever dream up. If I were to design a film version of

Tchaikovsky's *The Nutcracker* ballet, for the famous second act set in the Kingdom of Sweets, this is where I'd look for inspiration. Pamukkale, 'cotton castle' in Turkish, nicely reflects the area's traditional cash crop, but to an urban westerner whose most perfect white covering is the royal icing on a wedding cake, this is the ultimate in white icing. It's as though the whole 150-metre high hillside were iced and licked smooth, except for the areas where nature as master confectioner decided to have a little eccentric fun. She created deep shell-shaped bowls and staircases of shallow pools and little vertical sheer or plump, rounded cliffs, and she hung them about with bridal veils of delicate stalactites and scalloped edgings and frozen waterfalls. She roughed up the texture here and there for variety, even spending time on the fine sharp pleating you find on a circular species of coral or the undersides of mushrooms. It's all stark white on stark white. She filled the pools with warm spring water the intense, opaque pale blue of South Island river snowmelt, and in just a few places she allowed the black of the ancient earth beneath and the odd stubborn tree to remain visible, to throw the lacy glistening pristine whiteness into sharp, almost clinical contrast.

I stop near the top to drink in the clear air and the spectacular view of orange-roofed Pamukkale and the spring-green Meander river plain and snow-topped ranges beyond, and to paddle in some of the shell pools: a Kiwi among Germans, Turks, Canadians, but unlike them I'm troubled by a childhood memory, a painted image in childhood histories. I'm torn. I should not be allowed to be paddling like this. None of us should. I'm very grateful that I am, as no doubt the others are, photographing each other with their long-lens Nikons and tiny Sony videos. But it's wrong.

Once, on the other side of the planet, nature used silica and the power of a splendid geyser to create a fanlike staircase on the slopes above a lake named Rotomahana. The colours of this delicate and unique structure covering some three hectares were white, rose, coral, salmon, carnation, peach, russet, every possible shade of pink and warm pinky-brown. In 1886, she chose to obliterate those famous terraces with lava from the massive eruption of Mt Tarawera, and to drown them some years later one hundred and fifty metres under the waters of an expanded Rotomahana. Only some paintings and photographs remain, reminders of the fragility of the earth's crust, nature's ruthlessness, the impermanence of beauty.

The blue pools I'm standing in are naturally heated, some calf-deep and hot, some nearly empty and warm, and their bottom textures range from a thick white paste like face mask oozing up between my toes, to mosaics whose cracks indicate that the surface has begun to dry out and the calcium to harden. I try to walk precisely, only on the hard dry areas and the pools' firm flattened rims, where my feet will break up no mosaics and leave no imprint. And my inner voice is crying out, none of this should be here – neither people, nor the cigarette ends and empty packets, pyjama bottoms, silver film wrappings, single sneakers, plastic bags, old Band-aids and drink tins which twentieth-century people scatter carelessly behind them. There's little evidence of minders, or cleaners, or guardians of any sort other than two or three notices in Turkish, English and German telling you to remove your shoes. Today it's off-season, overcast and nippy.

There are maybe thirty people on the terraces; a school party arrives from Antalya, and I watch with interest and dismay as two of them, long-legged females in uniform slinky croptops quite inadequate for the conditions, stovepipe tight blue jeans and heavy-heeled black boots, stride from the bus and run fully booted across the white surface. Maybe fourteen, they shriek, and paw each other, and flaunt their admittedly gorgeous coltish bodies as do skiers on slopes. These are the class exhibitionists, Grade One bimbos. A young teacher does his ineffectual best to explain the no-shoes rule. They sit down on the edge of one of the pools – stiffly, gingerly, for those jeans are *tight* – and pick at the intricate laces on their boots only until teacher's attention is needed elsewhere, then blithely resume their jackbooted destruction of the upper blue pools. Teacher tries again, with even less effect, and again, to none. Eventually, maybe ten minutes later, a surly uniformed guard appears from drinking tea and they are harshly and loudly told either 'Boots off!' or 'Clear off!'

I can almost see the speech bubbles above their heads: Too difficult, too many laces and holes. Can't be bothered. Stupid rule. Stupid place. Stuff you. Stuff this white crap. Bor-ring! In Turkish, and probably in language to shock a Turkish sailor. They clear off back to the bus, glossed lips pouting, boots stamping, hair swinging. The parent and environmentalist in me both applaud their departure.

In another month, school parties and tourists from all over the world, for this is one of Turkey's most visited sites, will pour out of buses by their tens of thousands daily. Two million in a year will go padding around in their bare feet, swimming in the pools, breaking off the icicles either through carelessness or souveniring intent. They'll drop cigarette ends and pyjama bottoms and test the sleepy vigilance of the few on-duty watchmen and the maintenance workers who use pieces of corrugated iron, sheet plastic and stones to divert the precious hot waters down selected slopes.

The Kiwi in me, remembering the paintings and accounts of Tarawera's fury, looks around at the terraces now lit sparkling crimson by a spectacular setting sun far across the Meanderes plain and silently cries, 'A hundred years ago, we had no choice! Make yours and make it soon. If there must ever be any destruction here, let it not be by slow attrition, by man's greed and carelessness and insatiable appetite for amazement. Let only nature do it, by the way she has done it before, here at the city above and on the slopes of Mt Tarawera, by eruption or earthquake.'

A month later, back in New Zealand, I hear from Turkey that the hard call has been made, suddenly and without warning to the township. It's all over for tourists who dream of bathing romantically in the pools

Safeguarding the Cotton Castles

or taking the definitive picture of the terraces lit blood-red and apricot at sunset, or walking up from the village as I did in early morning to the sounds of goats' bells and the muezzin's call to worship. The quality of the sound broadcast across the valley from the small village mosque was, as so often anywhere in the Islamic world, intrusive, overly loud but halfway up the white path and in this magical God-given environment I was reminded, as intended, of my mortality and my reason to be grateful.

No more. The terraces have been closed, permanently. In 1988 the area was declared a World Heritage Park; in 1992 the Turkish government, supported by Unesco and the World Bank, announced with great fanfare that the terraces would be closed and the several brutally plain concrete motels along the crest, built in less ecologically-aware times, would be removed forthwith.

Five years of rumours and counter-rumours later – for this is Turkey, and Turkish central and local politics remind us of the derivation of the word byzantine – they are closing the terraces and removing the Pamukkale Motel surrounding the very hot, very sacred pool from which flow the mineral-laden waters that flow down across, and create, the terraces.

My son-in-law and daughter sound rightly worried. For those who run businesses in Pamukkale village itself, even for those whose shops are sited on the crest close to the foot traffic, it turns out to be a bad summer. Restaurants, hotels and those who sell T-shirts, film and guidebooks to tourists, are all hit hard. Tourists are not staying overnight in one of the village's nine hotels or thirty-five pensions, nor wandering down to the village for an evening meal and to buy souvenirs. Many buses are not coming down to the village at all; their passengers get out at the top of the terraces, take a few photos with their longest lenses, walk the two hundred metres up to the restored Roman theatre at nearby Hierapolis and drive away. For those who sell luxury items, like my son-in-law with his small but hitherto successful carpet shop, the summer is no better than they feared. For those who publish and sell vast quantities of guidebooks, postcards and posters, the sudden closure will eventually demand expensive reprinting, for all their current photographs feature the newly inadmissible: people.

This may be a mother's or an arrogant foreigner's wishful thinking, but I'm not overly gloomy about their future, nor that of Pamukkale as a tourist resort. Having a relatively short history of our own, even if taken from the earliest known Maori settlement of the twelfth century, I can't help but take a long view of theirs.

There have been prosperous settlements with Biblical names in this area for two thousand years or more: Hierapolis, Colossae, Aprodisias and Laodicae within a forty-kilometre radius of each other, Ephesus some two hundred kilometres away on the Aegean coast. These and others linked an important natural trade and military road between the Aegean world, the coastal cities of Ephesus and Smyrna (now Izmir), and the countries to the east. This road ran quite near where, around 190 BC, a city called Hierapolis was founded by Eumenes II, king of Pergamum, on a broad hillside plateau with unusually exuberant hot springs. From nearby established Laodicae, as far back as the third century BC, people travelled to the area to enjoy the waters; so many and so frequently that eventually they began to stay, and a city to rival Laodicae began to grow there.

By 133 BC Hierapolis had been conquered by the Romans. In AD 17, by which time Tiberius had succeeded Augustus to rule a prosperous Roman Empire approaching its zenith, the city was completely destroyed by earthquake. The Meanderes river valley is, after all, on a tectonic faultline. Another earthquake struck fifty years later, when Nero ruled. But Hierapolis rose again in the second century, becoming a major city noted across Asia Minor for its many fine temples, theatre, nearby marble mines, large Jewish community, stonecutters and metalworkers, carpets and fabrics, gardens of flowers and, yes, its health-giving thermal springs. Hadrian and (a hundred or so years later) Caracalla are believed to have visited.

Safeguarding the Cotton Castles

The golden age continued well into Byzantine times, but the writing was on the wall. One of the twelve apostles, St Philip, was crucified at Hierapolis in 80 AD; by the time of Constantine in the fourth century, Christianity was gaining wide acceptance in the city. He made the city capital of Phyrigia, but two hundred years later, for whatever reason, people were leaving. Travellers visiting in the 11th and 12th centuries, a dour period not noted for its pursuit of beauty and pleasure, mention nothing but ruins, a marble ghost town. Whatever settlement that had risen there by the Crusades of the 13th century was of little interest until finally Hierapolis was absorbed into the Ottoman Turkish empire, forerunner of the modern republic of Turkey.

Perhaps these centuries of neglect and desertion are the reason for the travertines' present extent and majesty. According to one writer, the waters of the thermal springs, left to run uncontrolled for so many centuries after the Roman and Byzantine periods, did indeed form the travertines that built up, the calcium carbonate deposit slowly invading an originally much steeper hillside, so that in certain places the city's remains are covered by travertines several metres high making excavation either impossible or difficult and uniquely different from any other ancient site. In the late nineteenth century there was enough interest in the ruins of Hierapolis stirring for the first excavations to be made. Amazingly, there was no further work done until the 1950s, when an Italian team began an ongoing association with the area of excavation, research and restoration.

Which brings us to modern Pamukkale and travertines that are now so precious they can only be wondered at, not walked on. In the last twenty or so years tourism has discovered Turkey. The small village that stood at the base of the travertines has become a modern tourist resort, ruthlessly seasonal. During winter, the hotels and shops are little patronised, or even close down completely. The village families go into hibernation or, like my son-in-law Beytullah and his New Zealand wife, flee to an antipodean summer to find work and buyers for their carpets. Traditionally his family, as do many Turks, went to Germany or elsewhere in eastern and central Europe to find work, but increasingly cheap air travel has now made it possible to look further afield.

Two grandmothers sharing a common pride – Hatice (pronounced Hati-jay) Özyurt (left) and Tessa Duder, with their three-month-old granddaughter Clare Sedef. This picture was taken on the day of the child's Turkish naming ceremony.

My Turkish family embodies the changes that are taking place in Turkish village society under the weight of international tourism. The men are all merchants and traders of one sort or another. A few of them own shops or hotels; others work for them, as whanau. They all speak enough of several languages – English, German, French, Italian – to sell carpets, some better than others. With one exception, none of the women speaks any other language at all. Not Beytullah's mother (in her fifties), nor his blind grandmother (seventies), nor his great-grandmother (nineties, maybe over a hundred, before she died late 1997), nor his great-aunt, nor his twenty-something sister-in-law. The exception is his teenage sister, who's an art student in Denizli and of that younger generation which is becoming, through CNN and the BBC World News on television and the influx of tourists and events like the Spice Girls playing Istanbul, speedily globalised.

They came, from a farming life, some with quite recent ties to Bulgaria and Syria, to live in Pamukkale because the town was fast becoming an international resort and there had to be opportunities for work there. From the 1960s, tourists on package tours involving round trips taking in Istanbul, Gallipoli, Ephesus, Bodrum, Marmaris, Pamukkale and Cappadocia, were arriving by their thousands. Hotels were built; thermal waters piped into swimming pools. Down side roads, some hotels remain unfinished, a reminder even in this idyllic hamlet of the appalling Turkish inflation rate (around 88 percent per annum) and as a consequence are literally thousands of unfinished buildings, mere concrete shells, littering the countryside and the urban landscape of modern Turkey.

My trip to Pamukkale from Istanbul also reminded me that not all modern travel has become easy. We had the option of a ten-hour bus ride from Istanbul, simple, cheap and, after a 28-hour air journey with a three-month old baby, exhausting. If connections could be made, we could take a forty-five-minute air flight to Denizli by a thrice-weekly Turkish Airlines (a short-haul RJ100, chunky and, I think, Russian-built) plus ninety minutes by car because the airport is well outside Denizli. Or we could take a 565-kilometre air flight to Izmir, about an hour, followed by a three-hour car trip about 200 kilometres inland.

It's axiomatic that the poorer the household, the warmer the hospitality. My daughter, her baby and I were given the warmest room, for was there not still light snow falling on the bare cherry trees outside? This room of the apartment was tiny. It contained the stove, the television, a birdcage, two sofas convertible to beds. Here the family, sitting on the floor, ate off a large circular tin tray. We shared breakfasts of small olives, white goats' cheese, fresh white bread and sweet Turkish tea, other meals of olives, chutneys, processed meats, bottled tomatoes and sweet plums, rice; and here, after much building up of the fire and re-arrangement of heavy cotton-padded embroidered bedding, I and my daughter and grandchild slept, almost too warmly. Grandmother, great-aunt and great-grandmother, round-busted serene old women whose faces and hands told of a lifetime of hard physical and domestic work, had been temporarily sent away to various relations. When I suggested that it would be easier for everyone if I took a room in a village motel, this was quickly quashed. Family stayed with family. Family looked after family. This is not a welfare state.

In the following two weeks, between spells of babysitting and drinking tea on family visits, I did the leisurely tourist number in and around Pamukkale. Buds were almost ready to burst on the cherry and pomegranate trees; shopkeepers were painting their shops; I heard new babies crying and spared a thought for their mothers trying to launder their babies' clothes, for the tap water here is as hard as expected, worse than post-war London, and leaves soap scum around basins and crusts inside kettles. I walked five times over the terraces, each time more entranced and in better weather than the last, although nothing prepares you for your first sighting – mainly because they are so much bigger than you imagine from photographs, covering maybe ten hectares along the hillside.

Now, should I go back to Turkey soon, I would not be able to walk and feel the terraces sensually with my hands and feet as I did in 1997. That unrestricted and enchanting pleasure is gone forever. Yet apart from the sheer visual experience, a remnant remains, sufficicent to take visitors close enough to experience the terraces at first hand. I'm told that the road up the right-hand flank remains open to foot traffic. They will charge you money at the bottom, and half-way up you will realise that the large blue pools you pass close by seem oddly symmetrical, in neatly ascending order, unnatural. So they are, being made of white concrete; a naive, crude attempt of a few years back to restore the damage made by the motor traffic up this road. I'm also told that in time these pools will become indistinguishable from the rest, for the waters are being, by those crude devices of corrugated iron and plastic sheets, diverted over these pools and are already forming crusted self-levelling lips to soften and blur the hard edges of concrete. In time, I was further told, the calcium deposits would have covered all the plastic bags and single sneakers and cigarette ends too. Swallowed them up. These cotton castles are alive!

While a diminished tactile pleasure remains, the grander visual one endures undiminished as it has done since the beginning of modern tourism. Yet, for all my enthusiasm, the travertines were not the absolute highlight of my time around Pamukkale.

Let me lead up to it slowly, for any Hellenistic or Roman ruin, be it in Italy, Greece or Turkey, is a place where you want to spend time, allowing your imagination to wander, ghosts to walk beside you, voices to call out and be heard.

Come with me first to the top of the terraces, by the legal route. It's about a ten-minute easy walk. Down to our left, note the majestic sweep of the travertines, levelling out into flat areas of cotton fields and the upper streets of Pamukkale town with its attractive orange-tiled roofs, its many trees, its hotels and swimming pools, its central plaza and narrow winding shop-lined roads so like Alpine skiing resorts.

Now at the top, 376 metres above sea level, note the delightful contrast between the blue and white terraces falling away beneath our feet and the peaceful pastoral scene below, a small township above an expansive river valley. We can spend a little time in the museum constructed beneath the well-preserved arches of the old Roman baths. Here are statues of Demeter, Greek goddess of fertility, and Triton the sea-god; friezes and columns and bas-reliefs and pots and coins and sarcophagi which have been found in the vicinity.

The ruins themselves, mostly from the Roman period, stretch over the hillside plateau as far along and up as you can see. We can wander along the main street, through the remains of a temple of Apollo and a building put up to honour the martyred St Philip, and see what's left of a street fountain, an arch of Domitian, the city walls, and a gate which dates from the Byzantine period. The whole hillside is thickly, impressively strewn with marble and stone pieces, and shepherds wearing cloaks of two whole sheepskins over not much else walk their goats through them in single file, little muted bells ringing.

There are three more attractions worth spending a good deal of time in. One is certainly the Roman theatre further up the hillside. It dates from the time of Hadrian, was used often up until the sixth century, was partly restored by the recent Italians and is capable of seating ten thousand people. The decorative details unearthed by the Italians are unusually well-preserved and the theatre's acoustics are miraculous. You can sit in the gods, thirty steeply raked rows up, and hear a whisper from the stage. Up here you can also get a magnificent panoramic view of the whole area, a ruined plateau and just a white crest where the travertines fall into the valley below.

The second is the necropolis, through which tour buses drive from the imposing, modern main gate, all steel and hard angles. This was a large and important burial ground even by Roman standards: traditionally they buried their dead on a road outside the city gates. Nowhere in Hierapolis do you get such a feeling of earthquake. Stone and marble, richly ornamented caskets, chamber tombs as big as small houses for whole noble families, and rounded tumulus graves for the poor, over a thousand of them here alone – all have been shifted, tilted, upended, their lids knocked off. Souls escaped, freed.

One hopes they travelled further than Hierapolis, for there's an ancient road to Hades here, the so-called Devil's Hole in the middle of a long, narrow terrace. Here poisonous gases escape from a cleft in the rock, along with the hot calcium-rich water which in less than two millennia has transformed this area. It's not safe even now; a locked metal gate and sign warns you of DANGER – POISONOUS GAS. The gas is carbon dioxide, and legends tell of priests who learned where pockets of fresh air lurked; appearing to defy nature, they could perform miracles.

Paradise is also to be found in this place, and it's the pool which was sacred to the Romans and is now the very best thing about Pamukkale. This is why tourists will continue to come to the area – yes, to marvel at the terraces and walk among the ruins, and best, to experience the supreme hot swim. New Zealanders know about the joys of thermal bathing – I've experienced their delights in Helensville, Waiwera, Miranda, Rotorua, Taupo, Tokaanu and Wairakei for starters – but Pamukkale is paradise.

Why? Forget the unprepossessing surroundings, the Pamukkale Motel around it which as I write is being demolished as part of the protection programme. Forget the outside air temperature of around 10 degrees Centigrade and the utilitarian dressing rooms. Forget everything. Walk down some stone steps into a pool fringed with pink oleander, roses, mulberry, hibiscus and cyprus trees and allow yourself to be transported utterly. For nowhere else, surely, can you float above the stumps of fallen Roman columns which once right here lined the main street of the city, and sit astride lengths of the very fluted marble columns once carved by their famed stonecutters.

Even without these marble fragments the pool, maybe some forty metres long and fifteen or so wide, would be appealing. With them, this pool is totally irresistible, like swimming in an intoxicating brew of alchemy and history. After two hours of exploring with my hands and feet the many columns, in lightly aerated water of perfect temperature (35 degrees Centigrade) and so rich in minerals that for two millennia claims have been made that it cures practically everything, my daughter and I were persuaded out only by the approach of grandchild's feed time.

The author in the historic hot pools of Pamukkale with their drowned marble ruins of the ancient Roman city of Hierapolis.

There is of course a local Cinderella legend which attests to the healing properties of the Pamukkale waters. Once upon a time, there was a girl so poor and ugly that when she became eligible for marriage and no one courted her, she determined to kill herself. She travelled to Pamukkale, and threw herself off the highest point of the terraces. But lo, she landed in a shallow pool, where eventually she was discovered by a passing prince from Denizli. She was still alive and so beautiful that, falling immediately in love, he took her home on his horse to his father's palace and married her.

Ah, me. Nothing much, it seems, changes, least of all romantic dreams of transformation. I believe I climbed out of the pool looking much as I did before, perhaps a little pinker, but I felt like a new woman for a few hours.

That night I took the immediate family to dinner in one of the hotels, to thank them for their hospitality. The transformation into smart suits, male and female, was startling, but the evening was not a great success. The baby, irritated by the smoke in the restaurant, cried and wouldn't settle, so her other grandmother, who'd made considerable efforts to dress for the occasion, nobly took her home early. I think they were nonplussed by my travelling (an older woman) alone and my fascination with walking on the terraces and amazed, even appalled, at how much a hot swim cost, and understandably quite unable to comprehend the length of the journey we made to get there or the sea-girt country my daughter and I came from. Some cultural leaps are just too wide even to attempt.

Since then I've done the tourist number around Waitomo, Taupo, Te Anau, Rotorua and Fiji, and seen them with new, insider eyes. I am newly polite to those who run businesses in these areas, especially as they look set to be in for a tough winter in 1998.

But our joint grandchild is what keeps us all going, in Turkey and in New Zealand. She's already a brown-eyed Turkish beauty, with absolutely no need to jump off the Pamukkale terraces. One of these days I'll take her for a swim in the Roman pool. We'll both sit astride the marble columns and that, my little one, will be paradise doubled.

Mexican Honeymoon

Michaelanne Forster

A Passion for Travel

I'VE BEEN TO Mexico twice, once as a girl and once with my husband. The first time I was an accomplice to murder and the second time I ended up divorced. All right, things were slightly more complicated than that but the moral of this travelogue is still pretty straightforward: the trip you plan is not always the trip you get.

I am nine years old and my family and all our luggage is jammed into a huge brown Ford station wagon the size of an army tank. We drive down the Pacific Coast Highway and cross the border at Tijuana where we're not allowed out of the car because it's too dirty and dangerous. Little children bang on the windows with their fists and try to sell us packs of Chiclets chewing gum. The murder happens on the desert road between Mazatland and Guadalajara. It's dusk and the car is hot and stuffy. There is nothing to see out the window but flat land and the occasional scraggly bush. Suddenly a cow steps in front of our car, seemingly out of nowhere. Whump! She flies onto the bonnet. My brothers and I sit bolt upright as bellowing rawhide, horns and hooves fill the front windscreen. Our mother screams, 'Don't stop, Mike, don't stop!' Dad accelerates and the car speeds away from the scene of the crime. The cow crumples onto the road. From the rear window of the station wagon I watch her get smaller and smaller until she disappears.

The next day we tour a pottery factory in Guadalajara. Then we go to an open-air market where my mother buys me a wooden peasant doll and some sandals called huaraches. My baby brother wanders off and he turns up at the local police station, returned there by a nice Mexican gentleman with a large moustache. All I can think about is the dead cow.

'Dad,' I say, 'Why did you kill that cow?'

'I didn't do it on purpose.'

'Why didn't you stop?'

'It wasn't safe. Anything could have happened.'

'Like what?'

'Like why don't you stop asking so many questions,' he says darkly. So I shut up. But I don't forget.

Bring the clock forward to the Christmas holidays in New Zealand thirty years later. My husband and I are planning our trip to Southern California the following July so that our children can see their grandparents and cousins. We're doing the dishes together and I'm thinking about a newspaper column I've read in the morning paper which says that the secret of a successful marriage is having fun together.

'Hey, let's go to Mexico,' I say brightly over a soapy casserole dish.

There's an interested silence from my husband.

'Just think. No family, no kids – a whole seven days to ourselves,' I wax on. I can see that he likes the idea of getting out of his family's clutches for a week so I volunteer to research the subject more thoroughly. Who knows? Maybe a short but glorious holiday together is exactly what we need to revive our flagging partnership.

A month later I've collected a stack of glossy brochures from California stuffed with breathless prose: 'Mexico is passion – a favourite destination for northern-hemisphere travellers who adore its Pacific and Gulf beaches, its fabulous archaeological sites and its vibrant culture ...' and so on. They don't mention southern-hemisphere travellers.

My husband looks at the brochures dubiously. He gets an atlas out of the bookshelf. 'July,' he says. 'Temperatures of 38 degrees in Oaxaca.'

'We could swim in the ocean to cool off.'

'Mazatland, Puerto Vallarta, San Felipe. All on the coast, all 48 degrees Celsius.'

'Are you saying you don't want to go?'

'I'm saying if we go we need to find a place that isn't like the inside of a pizza oven,' he replies.

Fair enough. We settle on the highlands of central Mexico, a region almost as big as France, which takes in six states. We decide that the centre state, Guanajuato, looks good. As the birthplace of Mexican independence it promises 'charming colonial architecture', museums, monuments and reasonably temperate weather. Whatever happens, at least we won't cook.

I sign up for Spanish lessons with a disgruntled Argentinian who drills me on irregular verbs I once knew and now have forgotten. The language sets off a cavalcade of faces and names I haven't thought of for years. Marguerita Clavaria. Anita Ybarra. Maria Lopez. Roberto Barrio. They're at school, permanently parked at the back of the classroom. Nobody tells me they don't speak English so I just think they're dumb. Why does Manuel wear a crucifix and have a gold-capped tooth? Why do Anita and Marguerita have pierced ears? My mother has told me, very plainly, that nice little girls don't wear earrings. I'm confused. Why do the Mexican boys sweat and crash around the circle in the wrong direction, stepping on my toes with their pointy black shoes when we do square dancing? Why do the girls wear those awful cotton dresses and tie their black plaits together with white ribbons? Some of them have started to sprout breasts. What are they doing in our classroom? We're still little kids.

Roberto and Manuel are greasers, I think. Greasers. Greasers. Their hair is so oily that comb marks run through it like furrows of a plough.

'I want to confess something,' I say to my husband one morning in June.

'What's that?'

'When I was little we called Mexican kids names,' I say. 'We treated them like shit.'

He shows me a magazine article that says California has two million illegal immigrants, over half of them from Mexico. Now that I'm grown-up I realise you don't leave your homeland and sneak over the border of another country for the fun of it. Poor Marguerita, poor Manuel. I hope they're selling computer software or arguing cases before the Supreme Court, but I suspect they're not. I think about explaining the context of the confession to my husband but I don't. He's busy with heart-attack patients, sore throats and an unexpected outbreak of gout – and then it's July and the second honeymoon is upon us.

We board an Aero Mexico plane in Los Angeles for Querétaro, the nearest city to our first destination, San Miguel de Allende. Knees touching, we take off. The plane is full of Mexicans. All the overhead lockers are bursting with American clothes, toys and household goods. Everybody seems buoyant. The food is good and the toilets are fully functioning. We could be going anywhere, really – Paris, Rome or Tokyo. Only the mariachi music over the intercom gives our destination away.

Four hours later we are in Mexico. We board an almost empty

Michaelanne Forster

tourist bus. I choose a seat on the left-hand aisle and my husband chooses one on the right. It's one of those telling moments that, in retrospect, probably say it all. We pass a rubber factory, a shoe factory, gas tanks and tumbledown buildings that may be warehouses. The bus driver turns on the radio and a steady stream of cheap music pours out of it. 'Querida, te amo, te quiero, todos los dias (My dear I love you, I want you everyday)'. Oh yeah, I think sourly.

The landscape looks like Southern California. It's scorched and eroded but I know we're in Mexico because there's a farmer with a burro walking alongside the two-lane highway. Nothing much happens. I stay glued to my window and my husband stays glued to his. I see some women and children squatting outside a wretched adobe house. It's not picturesque, vibrant or even faintly colourful. What have I got us into?

The bus lets us off on the outskirts of the town. We decide to walk to our hotel because we're on a tight budget and we don't want to get ripped off by a taxi driver on the first day of our second honeymoon. Children stare at us and old women in black give us the evil eye from their front porches. Skinny dogs and children roam the streets; chickens peck listlessly at non-existent grass. The land of milk and honey it is not. We keep walking.

Suddenly we're in the middle of an olde-worlde Spanish travel poster. The streets are narrow and cobbled, the houses thick-walled and palatial in scale. Doors are ornately carved and windows are surrounded by ornamental wrought-iron. The town glows with colour – golden ochre, creamy white, dusky pink. I'm so relieved I could cry.

We dump our backpacks at the hotel, amazed by its luxury. Our room has a high ceiling, thick adobe walls, cool tile floors and huge windows. There are even two double beds. Will the passion of Mexico send us tumbling between the sheets, first in bed number one and then in bed number two?

It does not.

That afternoon we explore the central plaza. It's full of costumed musicians strumming guitars, serenading hapless tourists. There are street vendors everywhere, many of them children, hawking cheap toys, balloons, jewellery, junky 'folk art' and sweets. Surrounding the plaza are banks, restaurants, ice-cream parlours, tourist shops, a bizarre baroque church and a museum. We find a restaurant close to the main square and sit down to order our meal. No sooner has the waiter placed a basket of bread on our table than three little children appear. They point at the bread with huge soulful eyes.

'Tengo hambre, por favor, Señora.' I'm hungry, Missus.

It's hopeless. I think of my own children and give them bread and money. 'That's not going to change anything,' says my husband.

I know he's right but I never get used to seeing those tiny bare feet and outstretched hands. They are everywhere we go.

Retired Americans are everywhere we go as well. The noticeboard

at the Bellas Artes Centre, a beautiful former convent now run by the government as a kind of cultural clearing house, is full of signs (in English) advertising coffee mornings, Shiatsu massage and photography classes.

'We just love it here,' exclaims a tall, elegantly dressed woman well past sixty. She is talking to a group of tourists, my husband and me included, who have descended on her house as part of a house-and-garden tour sponsored by local expatriates. The Americans bond with each other: 'You're from Duluth? I've got an aunt in Minnesota.' Outside, the narrow dusty streets are crowded with people, old cars and buses. Inside it's quiet and cool, as the houses are built of mud brick and plaster to provide protection from the continuous heat.

'Look,' says my husband, nudging me in the ribs. We're in the next expatriate domain where a Mexican maid is dusting a large collection of framed photos – Christmas, a son's graduation, a baby granddaughter's first step.

'If you retired down here you'd miss so much of your family's day-to-day life,' I whisper.

'Yeah,' he replies. 'Wouldn't that be great?' We move to a flower-filled patio with a tinkling fountain, tasteful Mexican objets d'art and a gardener clipping back the bougainvillea. Getting good help is obviously not a problem.

The next day takes us on a walking tour where we learn that the town is named after Ignacio Allende who conspired, in 1810, to end Spanish rule with Father Miguel Hidalgo. Both men were executed, says our guide. His English is excellent and he sounds bored. He tells me he worked in San Diego for two years at Taco Bell. I decide not to ask if he was legal.

By the third day my poor command of Spanish and my husband's non-existent one sees us sinking into our own little tourist bubble. We sit facing one another in a restaurant looking for things to say. He informs me, with all the courage of a medical man, that he is going to eat a salad. He is sick of beer, tortillas, beans and meat. 'I have the kind of stomach that can take anything,' he says.

I don't argue. It's his stomach. I have been careful not to eat any fresh greens or fruit or drink unbottled water but somehow, somewhere, the bacteria is invading. (My brother tells me later the water I drank from the carafe the hotel maid so kindly left at my bedside in San Miguel was probably filled from an unfiltered tap out the back.)

We head into the capital city of Guanajuato, a bustling university town with a strong cultural and artistic history. I think I'm getting the hang of travelling in Mexico. I'm slowing down. I'm getting used to waiting and letting things unfold in their own sweet time.

'We could go see the house where Diego Rivera was born,' I suggest to my husband as the bus takes us through the crazy urban canyons (los callejones) that lace the city. Or else the Basilica of Our Lady of Guanajuato. It's got a statue of the Virgin –'

Mexican Honeymoon

'All that Mary-worshipping gives me the creeps,' says my husband.

'The statue's really old. From King Philip of Spain.'

'Yeah, right,' he replies. 'Let's get to the hotel first.'

We're in the central square this time but the room is barely the size of a walk-in closet and I'm not in the mood to search for something better. In fact all I want to do is lie down on the bed and have a sleep. Or maybe I'm hungry – I know something isn't right but I can't put my finger on it.

My husband goes off to sightsee and I eat lunch at an open-air café outside the hotel. No sooner do I lift my fork to my mouth than three musicians in sombreros and sequins appear. If I hear another bar of soppy Mexican music I'll go mad. They begin to play and I try to ignore them, pushing the beans around on my plate while I daydream about asparagus, peaches and watermelon.

Fifteen minutes later I'm shitting my guts out. The onset of Montezuma's Revenge is sudden and terrible. After a brief shooting pain in your gut, your bowels open almost instantaneously and every molecule of food and water that you ever consumed in your life comes flooding out. When my husband returns to the hotel room several hours later, I'm on the floor somewhere between the toilet and the bed, utterly exhausted.

'Do you have anything in your first-aid kit?' I gasp.

'No,' he says. 'It's better to let the bugs out.'

'Maybe that's what the medical books say, but if I don't get some kind of pharmaceutical plug there's not going to be anything of me left.'

He loyally sets off to find a pharmacia and returns with some Lomotil, an anti-diarrhea medicine. The afternoon crawls on and the music in the plaza outside becomes more and more insistent. I fall asleep. Hours later I wake up to hear my husband retching his guts out. Now we're both on the toilet, one after the other. Together at last, I think.

We wake up again and find it's past midnight. The music is reaching its zenith and the corridor outside our hotel room is like a train station. Lift doors disgorge one lot after another of inebriated hotel guests, all fantastically noisy and jolly. We ring the hotel desk for bottled water. Some might have come, hours later. I don't remember.

The next morning my husband manages to change our air tickets so that we can leave the following day at noon. They're standby tickets only, but there's nothing else available. 'It's now or never,' he says. 'We've got to get back to Querétaro by late afternoon or we'll be stuck here another three days.'

'I can't travel like this,' I say. I'm on the floor again, crawling from the toilet to the bed. I don't think I can walk without fainting.

My husband stands over me, half-pleading, half-demanding. He looks heroic, like a soldier about to drag his wounded comrade from a muddy trench. 'Come on,' he says. 'Get up.'

'But this is supposed to be our second honeymoon,' I cry.

He doesn't answer. He's probably too sick.

All the way back to Los Angeles I think only two thoughts: dear God may I not shit myself in public, and something is wrong that is not going to be fixed the way I want it to be.

Back in Newport Beach my husband's family is very sympathetic. 'How disappointed you must be,' they say, 'to have your wonderful romantic holiday ruined by illness.' I smile, pale and wan. There's no point in ruining their illusions.

The Lomotil stops the worst symptoms (although we don't fully recover for another three or four weeks) so my husband decides to book an early flight home to New Zealand. 'You can stay here with the kids, but I'd just as soon get back to work and take some time off later to go skiing.'

'Okay,' I say. I don't ski.

I try not to be disappointed but I am. I was probably stupid to suggest the trip in the first place. You can't make a honeymoon when there's no honey and no moon, right? All that 'passion of Mexico' stuff is just a sell-job anyway. A tourist illusion.

'How was your trip?' everyone asks when I get back to Christchurch. I sketch, in a few amusing paragraphs, my story of our exotic holiday together and its swift and sudden ending. Two months later we separate. I don't know how my husband remembers Mexico. It's never come up as a topic for discussion. He says he doesn't know where the photos of the trip are. Maybe he's burned them, but more likely they never got developed.

It's strange but what I remember best is Mexico the first time around with the cow crumpled on the road getting smaller and smaller until she disappears.

Eight Days *in* Antarctica

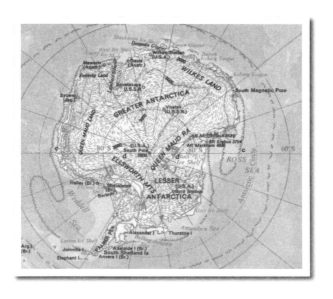

Chris Orsman

THE FROST-RIMED oval of the Hercules window emitted an intense glare. As I approached and stared out, the window seemed to frame a fleeting image of Earth itself as seen from space, all glacier and snow and ocean – an ice planet. Cape Adare lay off our port wing, a white horn in a sea of Delft dusted with fine floes like icing sugar. Along the Cape there was a confusion of small bays and grey-blue cliffs. A whitish haze hung over the horizon. My eyes began to water with the brightness of the vision and I drew back into the dim belly of the plane. In another hour we would be landing on the McMurdo Ice Shelf.

Antarctica is usually off-limits to travellers for various practical reasons. Not many can afford the expense of private expeditions, or the high cost of cruises in ice-strengthened tourist boats. Travel there is almost always privileged travel. But this perhaps is changing a little. In the summer of 1998 I went to Antarctica with Bill Manhire and Nigel Brown. We formed, in effect, the 'expeditionary force' of the new Artists to Antarctica programme, the brainchild of Tim Higham, communications manager of Antarctica New Zealand. We were also accompanied by a film crew who were making a documentary of the trip. We spent eight-and-a-half days in the Antarctic; we camped at Lake Bonney in the Taylor Valley, and visited historic sites at Cape Royds, Cape Evans, and Hut Point. We experienced the hospitality of Scott Base and visited the Americans at McMurdo Station.

Antarctica attracts hyperbole: you will hear it described as the highest, driest, coldest, windiest place on earth. It must surely be the healthiest place too, if you consider the proscribed list of conditions that appear on the medical examination: asthma, diabetes, high blood pressure, to name a few. Applicants are thoroughly screened to identify risk factors, to ensure that they are 'free from incipient disease or functional impairment'. Teeth must also be in good repair. Fortunately, we were spared the rigorous winter training course at Lake Tekapo that two years earlier was mandatory for first-time Antarcticans: it would have seen us building igloos and crawling through smoke-filled huts wearing breathing apparatus.

Our trip was scheduled for January 19-27, the warmest time of the Antarctic year. I booked myself on the Cook Strait ferry and the Picton-Christchurch train, for I had decided to follow my grandfather's route south when he went to visit the *Terra Nova*, Captain Scott's vessel, in the spring of 1910.

I travelled light: backpack, face-mask and earplugs, camera and film, notebook, pencils and sharpener, half a box of Havana cigars (Montecristo No 4s, supplied by my friend Peter Zwart from a recent trip to Cuba), US and New Zealand dollars, boxes of windproof matches, a small Bible, a torch and reading material. As well as clothes and toiletries, I included a book-making kit, for one of my projects was to publish a small book of poems in Antarctica.

As we sailed out of Port Nicholson on the Saturday, three orcas appeared off the starboard side and accompanied the ferry for a spell. This seemed an auspicious start to the adventure. *Spiceworld* was playing in the small theatrette on board, and the ferry was packed with tourists and holidaymakers. I entrained at Picton and was soon in the heart of drought-ridden Marlborough which looked like an Oklahoma dust bowl. A white heat seemed to hang over the hills, along with the glare of parched grass. The saltworks and panned lakes of Lake Grassmere passed by like snowfields, and then there was the relief of the summer sea, a deep Prussian blue under the ranges. North Canterbury was also parched, but the glare was relieved by windbreaks and clustered trees which threw a shadowed coolness across roads and railway tracks. Morning tea was announced and then served, along with a rather gauche emphasis (repeated) that those in the 'backpackers' carriage' were not entitled to any. I anticipated something home-made and generous: it turned out to be two cellophaned biscuits and weak coffee.

We met at the International Antarctic Centre the following Monday to get kitted up. A large pile of clothing and footwear awaited each of us. We stripped down to our underpants and donned, piece by piece, the body armour of Antarctica: socks, longjohns, thermal salopettes, woollen shirt, windproof salopettes, windproof vest, neck gaiter, and survival jacket, along with balaclavas and headgear, goggles and mittens. We tried on our Mukluks – a modern version of an Eskimo snow boot – and Sorrels, fur-lined Canadian boots. We were each issued with a pair of metal dogtags stamped with our names and blood types.

One of the features of Antarctic travel is its uncertainty. Flights are loosely scheduled and are very much subject to the vagaries of the weather. Our Tuesday morning flight was rescheduled to Wednesday. The 'flight' came to assume an inflated importance during those summer days as we readjusted our schedule and filled in the time sightseeing, visiting galleries, museums and the Botanic Gardens.

By Wednesday we were getting anxious to be away. We filled in the morning with a long walk along the cliffs at Taylor's Mistake and drove over to Lyttelton for lunch, with the funnels and gantries of the port as a backdrop. Tim phoned the Movements Controller and we learned that the flight had again been delayed a day. We returned to the International Antarctica Centre and pottered around the library for a few hours. I watched a video of *Scott of the Antarctic*. This was not life as I had imagined it in the deep South and I used the fast-forward liberally. I stayed that night at Tim Higham's place and slept dreamlessly under a large poster of the Spice Girls.

The morning of departure, Thursday 22 January, was mild and slightly overcast, with a light northerly blowing. We arrived at the passenger terminal of the International Antarctic Centre just before eight o'clock and checked in our baggage. Everything was weighed, even the passengers. An enthusiastic drug dog sniffed our bags; Tim was worried that my Havana cigars would be discovered and confiscated.

After a late breakfast at the US Navy cafeteria *Southernlights*, we made our way back to the departure lounge for an Antarctic safety video which seemed designed to key-up already nervous travellers rather than reassure them. The helicopters came across as particularly menacing, with the threat of decapitation. A heavy American accent started the video with Captain Scott's famous words at the Pole: 'My God this is an awful place.' Several bad imitations passed round the changing room as we put on our survival gear for the flight. At 9.30 we were bussed out to the American air base and boarded the Hercules. We were finally airborne at 10.23.

What we had heard and imagined about Hercules flights, and what we experienced, were rather different things. We had built up a grim picture from various sources; the reality was something of a relief. The LC-130 Hercules (ski-equipped) seemed a bit of a flying whale. The passenger cabin was about twelve metres long and three-and-a-half metres high, with ducting and other viscera running along the ceiling and walls. Slung harnesses above formed sleeping hammocks for off-duty crew. A long row of hand baggage was strapped down in the middle of the cabin. We were each handed a paper bag bulging with fruit and vegetable salads, meat rolls, American soft drink and chocolate bars, and strapped ourselves into the webbing and canvas seats that ran along both sides of the cabin.

There were twenty-five passengers on board, with the strident red jackets of the Americans predominating over the blues and yellows of the New Zealanders. The noise of the engines was too loud to talk over; we put in our ear plugs and communicated by body language and hand signals. We settled down to reading, sketching and dozing, with occasional trips to the rear to gaze out the windows. Toilet facilities, also at the rear, were minimal: for the gentlemen, a tin funnel over a barrel; for the ladies, a 'honey-bucket' – a plastic bucket with toilet seat and lid. This was not an item hotly in demand. A shower curtain had been strung up to give a modicum of privacy.

After about five-and-a-half hours' flight we saw our first icebergs floating like polystyrene on the mild blue Southern Ocean. The heating in the plane was cut to help us acclimatise. Jackets and vests went back on as the cabin cooled. About an hour and a half later we flew over the Antarctic coast.

We touched down on Willy's Field at 6.39 in the evening, after an eight-and-a-half hour flight. As the passengers queued to disembark I watched the cargo door slowly open and Mt Erebus, cone-first, descend into view. A small plume of smoke drifted off the summit forty kilometres away. The mountain, 3794 metres high, dominates Ross Island. Among New Zealanders on the ice there seems to be a tacit agreement not to make too much of Mt Erebus: everyone understands its associations. At any rate, as we stood blinking on the sea ice at Willy's Field and marvelled at the expanse and clarity of our surroundings, the mountain seemed a symbol of the continent itself. None of us had words to match what we saw.

We were met on the field by Rex Hendry, operations manager at Scott Base, and driven off in Toyota pickups. The route was marked by flagged poles and we stopped halfway to let the film crew drive ahead and set up various shots of our arrival. I looked towards Mt Erebus. A belt of cloud was moving swiftly across it from the west; soon the mountain and middle distance were effaced, wiped clean. All spatial reference, depth of field, proportion, texture and shape, were vanishing in the white-out. It was an eerie sight. I pointed it out to Bill and Nigel, and we stood silently watching the cloud obliterate the mountain and the background of Ross Island.

Scott Base is situated at the southern extremity of Ross Island. The base is New Zealand's southernmost port of call, a small colony of green huts interlinked with sealed corridors, standing on the foreshore of Pram Point. The green colour of the huts was apparently chosen by Robert Thompson, a long-serving superintendent of the Antarctic Division, to invert the sequence of white cottages among the green fields of England – or so the local folklore has it. The base is exquisitely sited, and the panoramas across the McMurdo and Ross ice shelves are impressive. White Island and the low dark cliffs of Black Island lie directly south; a little further west lies Brown Peninsula, terminating with the distinctive cone of Mt Discovery. The architecture of the base is completely functional. The huts are clad in vertical sheeting, with roofs at a shallow pitch. All the exterior doors are adapted from commercial freezers. The atmosphere inside seemed a cross between a superior youth hostel and an alpine lodge. We took to its low-key format and immediately felt at home there.

That evening we settled into our quarters in Q Hut, which holds summer accommodation, labs, library and gymnasium. Bill and I shared a narrow cubicle lit by a window with small internal shutters. We unpacked and made a quick tour of the base, along with many introductions, then had a late dinner of pasta and salad, finishing off with a few drinks in the bar. The duty-free prices made it a cheap evening.

I wandered down to the shore after dinner to smoke one of my Havanas. The sea ice had broken under the tide and a large channel of water had opened up. A Minke whale surfaced and cruised briefly along the sound. A wind of ten knots or so reduced the ambient temperature to about minus fifteen as I smoked my cigar contentedly, chatting with the film crew who were recording the scene. 'This one is for the Pope,' I joked, referring to John Paul's recent visit to Cuba. After a few minutes my gloveless hand grew numb and heavy: the precursor to frostbite. I plunged it deep under my arm to warm it up, having endured a short sharp lesson in Antarctic safety.

A group photograph taken the next morning on the foreshore of Pram Point shows a well-shaven, slightly sun-struck group of neophytes all on something of a high. This was partly novelty and excitement, partly the amount of information that was pouring down on us. We had our first briefing at nine o'clock – which covered everything from recycling to helicopter safety, as well as more esoteric material and local folklore. We learned, for example, that someone had calculated that the bodies of Scott and his companions broke out of the ice shelf into the Ross Sea in 1967.

Field training is now tailored to need. After a three-hour classroom session we were taken to one of the workshops to familiarise ourselves with the primus and other camping gear. We were shown how to erect our polar tents, the circular, double-layered nylon igloos with which we would soon become very familiar.

At two o'clock we were loaded onto a RNZAF Iroquois, together with a mountain of equipment. Helicopters (helos) are the workhorses of the Antarctic and carry a quite astonishing payload. My main memory of crossing the sea ice over McMurdo Sound is a pair of purple fluffy dice hanging from the cabin of the helicopter. Forty minutes after take-off we landed at Lake Bonney in the Taylor Valley.

The Taylor Valley, one of the famous 'Dry Valleys' of the Antarctic, is about forty kilometres long. It lies on a north-east, south-west axis, terminating at New Harbour in McMurdo Sound. Lake Bonney lies at its other extremity, a curving lake about five kilometres long, intersected by the spur of the Bonney Riegel.

Our campsite was superbly sited at the western end of the lake, at a place named Blood Falls after the curious rusty staining on the glacier face caused by ferrous compounds. Various glaciers met at Lake Bonney like points of the compass. To the north, the Rhone Glacier spilled over a ridge half a kilometre up the mountain side; its terminal face was pointed like an arrow, with flattened skirts of crumbled ice on all sides. To the south was Sentinel Peak, 2400 metres high, and the Calkin Glacier. The most impressive of all was the massive Taylor Glacier. Its terminal face, twenty metres high, dominated the campsite, running westwards as far as the eye could see. The valley funnelled to its narrowest point at Blood Falls, and the surface of the glacier here was serrated and buckled, like water forced into a narrow turbulent channel. Our campsite was also close to a noisy river that ran beneath the north face of the glacier. A smaller stream flowed down from the Rhone Glacier and we were never far from the sound of running water.

The Taylor Glacier is about fifty kilometres long and shaped like a wide, serifed U. It steps up on sloping plateaus, broken by crevasses and ice falls, to the Polar Plateau. The Katabatic winds that flow, very dense and cold, off the plateau and down the glaciers sluice the Dry Valleys free of snow and promote an exceptionally low humidity.

We were there for four nights. A field party of glaciologists had pitched their cluster of blue and yellow tents a month or so earlier. A column of stones, like a Tibetan *chorten* or tomb, marked the helo

Working out the polar tent: Bill Manhire at Cape Royds.

landing pad. This primitive structure made quite an impression, suggesting the stoic remains of some ancient race long departed from the valley. We had plenty of time to observe our surroundings. And plenty of daylight too. The sun shone for twenty-four hours of the day, circling us at a low angle of about 35 degrees. Soon after midnight it passed behind the Kukri Hills, a range of mountains along the south axis of the valley, with peaks rising between 1300 and 2200 metres. The camp was in shadow for six hours, the temperature dropped and the ice thickened on the shore of the lake.

The colouring of the valley, and to some extent its texture, reminded me of the panoramas taken of the Martian surface by remote-control spacecraft. There was the suggestion everywhere of a light reddish brown permeating the greys and whites of granite, marble, quartz. The valley was strewn with boulders and rock of all sizes, casting deep shadows in the low sun. I have a photograph of us sitting atop a huge boulder three or four metres in height. But it was difficult, from any point of vantage, to determine the size and distance of things. All the normal registers of scale – trees, houses, small hills, wildlife – were absent. What might appear as a small boulder a hundred metres off would turn out to be something huge a kilometre away. The clarity of the air probably had some part in this. The human form, itself a rarity in that landscape, was the only useful determinant of scale, apart from the tents of the campsite.

It struck me that the stone in the valley would provide excellent building material. The elements of structure were all around: rock weathered and shaped into rough tiles and slates, boulders flattened to a suggestion of ashlar. It would not have been difficult to erect dry-stone walling of reasonable fit.

The lake was a constant focus, a lens in our unique ecosystem. It was a literal lens in that the surface of the lake (four metres thick at its densest) focuses the sun and warms the water below. But it was also a lens in the sense of an imaginative focus, concentrating energies of a different kind and sharpening the inner eye. That sharpness was also matched by the constant sense of an edge to things – the spine of the mountain ranges, the facets of the glacier itself, the piercing wind. There was a balance to this. I consult my journal and find this response:

> There are other contours, too, rounded shapes and outlines that can be described by the extravagant sweep of the arm from the elbow, or the sine waves formed by the hand: organic contours, the ogee line of beauty. Here, under a ventifact boulder, in the shade of a small gully, the

human scale is restored. Our muffled shapes – padded, foamed, layered with survival clothing – at times seem a natural part of the scene, traipsing the valley floor or climbing onto the surrounding slopes. The strident blues and yellows of our gear stand out in bold counterpoint to the greys and reddish browns of the valley. Above us, the arc of a mountain ridge bends under the weight of the sky.

The lyrical stood alongside the earthy, and the contemplative silence was often qualified. The lake, for example, had an interesting repertoire of sounds and was quite unpredictable in its gurgling, rumbling and farting, like an embarrassing dinner guest. The cliffs of the glacier would collapse thunderously; sometimes we heard the rending and cracking of ice, like a tearing of huge branches. At other times, when we walked along the shore or into the hills, the silence was complete. We heard only the systole of the heart.

What did we do there? A lot and a little. Nigel was a hive of industry from the first. Within an hour of arrival his easel was set up and he was busy painting and sketching. And talking! He proved a natural for the camera, a welcome deflection for the more camera-shy among us, providing a continual commentary on painting and art and life in general.

Nigel's output and energy were prodigious. He soon abandoned his easel and painted on the ground, pinning his canvasses down with stones. He seemed to paint and sketch everything. He even painted the preserved seal that had crawled up the valley some fifty or a hundred years before and lay mournfully a stone's throw from the campsite. While he painted, he conversed with it.

There was one dramatic moment when he asked me to sit for a sketch. I held a pose, staring across at the glacier face. I was telling him about how writing prose in the Antarctic seemed rather boring, how it seemed more a poet's landscape, when a huge slab of the glacier fell off right before my eyes. The detonation roused everyone in camp. Nigel penned this couplet below his sketch:

> Orsman said prose seemed boring,
> then the glacier started falling ...

Yes, Nigel wrote poems too. Tim Higham, who shared a tent with him, complained mildly about his composing aloud at two in the morning. But the talking was not confined to Nigel: there was plenty of joking, banter and genial insult – the sort of thing, I imagine, that went on in Scott's hut. Bill proved to be a superb mimic and could imitate almost any poet you named. His Yeats and Sam Hunt were particularly good. Hearing 'The Lake Isle of Innisfree' quoted beside a remote Antarctic lake in Yeats's lilting Irish was an experience to remember.

The poets were busy, too, though in a more laconic fashion. Behind all the daily activity – the larking about, the long walks, the sitting and contemplating, eating and drinking and yarning – the serious business of 'data retrieval' was in hand. The isolation of our surroundings helped this process. Everything around us was reduced to elementals – heat and cold, wind and calm, sun and cloud – and distractions were minimal. There was ordinarily little sense of smell. Insect life was totally absent: turn over a stone and there were no spiders or slaters; no wetas crawled into our sleeping bags; no flies or mosquitoes bothered us in the evenings. The only other living thing, apart from ourselves, was a dark lichen that we found in a dry river bed on the mountain side.

Bill kept a small pocket notebook and would often stop and jot something down. He was very alert to the language of the place, the technical terms of the glaciologists, geographic names, things incongruous, impressions voiced by the party, the way in which the ordinary was constantly charged with the extraordinary. Small things took on significance. For instance, one day we crossed the lake and climbed up into the Kukri Hills. It was a tramp of some hours during which we discovered a rusty canister, part of a parachute flare dropped by an aircraft. An ordinary piece of junk in New Zealand, it was treated as a rare and interesting find in the Taylor Valley.

Paint and words also came together. Nigel was keen to gather quotes from the poets for his canvasses and to get them down in paint at their place of origin. I remember one morning in particular when we woke up to find the camp under snow. It was overcast and very cold. Nigel was up soon after eight o'clock and painting hard. Every now and then he brushed snow off his canvas. His painting-water froze and warm water was brought from the primus. It was a scene of single-minded dedication where text and paint came together naturally, arising out of a shared experience of the place. One picture was named after Bill's poem 'Gust of Light'. The other was called 'The Lakes of Mars', from my field poem of the same title:

The Lakes of Mars

Primed to silence, the valley
magnifies the crack of the lake
to the glory of God. You climb
a saddle of low hills
and hear the wind's soft boom
across the ears; you see
the mountains' rim,
shadow-trailing boulders:
the planet's edge
hones nerves and heart.

The course of a private sun
caught in the first circle
defines the place; you ask
how deep is your valley

> where the winds lifts nothing
> larger than a pebble. Your tracks
> remain, weathering slowly;
> the place will ignore
> the ribbed print of boots.
> Under the tent's fawn glow
> waken to Antarctica.
> Open the flaps: night glares
> over glacier and rusty falls.

Mike Single, Jeannie Ackley and James Bellamy, the film crew, were also kept busy. Their brief was to record our peculiarities and interactions and they were most assiduous in this, becoming very much a part of the group. Nigel, of course, was a natural performer, ever busy at his work and a godsend for the camera. The poets were harder put to look useful and inspired. We did what we could, reading for the camera (and once, over the RT, for the Concert Programme's *Bookmarks* programme in Christchurch). The poetry was straight from its source, not much revised. The hardest part was probably maintaining meaningful conversations when we knew we were being filmed.

We were helped a lot by the glaciologists. Bryn, Ange and Brian were busy on a project to measure the rate of flow of the Taylor Glacier. The work was arduous and risky. Brian would abseil down the glacier face to take core samples. Angela and Bryn would work right under the glacier face, cutting pieces off. At times the din of the chainsaw echoed around the campsite and up and around the valley, incongruous and familiar in a kind of Gothic way. Our conversations together, sitting around the primus in the common tent, or out in the sunshine of an evening, were of real mutual interest and possibly provided some of the best footage of its kind for the camera.

One morning we learned the astonishing news that the Governor-General and Lady Hardie Boys were to visit the campsite at Blood Falls.

Apparently each new governor-general visits the ice to underscore our sovereignty over the Ross Dependency. Blood Falls had been chosen for a brief field visit.

We lingered around camp that morning, waiting for the throb of the helo at the end of the lake, standing unshaven and unwashed and gawking like the proselytes of a cargo cult as the Iroquois descended and the immaculate vice-regal party disembarked. There were introductions all round, handshakes, and mutually polite conversation before the official party headed up the glacier to find the scientists, leaving a lingering smell of cologne. Lady Hardie Boys made her way to the lakeside to do some quiet sketching. After a time, we brewed a plunger of coffee and went down to join her. It was all most pleasant and informal. When the helicopter arrived back to pick up the party, the wind from the rotor blades blew Lady Hardie-Boys' pencil case away. Nigel and I distinguished ourselves by dashing onto the lake to retrieve it, a gallant finale.

We were due to be lifted out of the valley on Tuesday afternoon. The film crew had booked extra helicopter time and for an hour and a half we flew up the Taylor Glacier and over the terrain bordering the Polar Plateau. We circled the western slopes of the Asgard and Olympus Ranges, the Wright Upper Glacier and the extraordinary formations of the Labyrinth Dais. If the sublime has been defined as 'curiosity ting'd with terror' then the sight of the Polar Plateau was sublime indeed. We flew out onto this vast ice ocean at a height of 2500 metres, with our starboard door removed for the camera. The Plateau seemed endless and minatory, curved with the curve of the earth itself.

We touched down at Cape Royds on Ross Island later that afternoon. The Cape hosts the world's southernmost Adélie penguin colony, and is also the site of Shackleton's hut, base of the 1907 *Nimrod* expedition. There was a marked contrast between this place of historic and natural interest, and the comparative quiet and emptiness of the Taylor Valley. Firstly, there was the penguins' high officiating chatter as a constant background noise. There seemed to be a continuous party going on in the rookery, which was large and odorous. The smell was like a shrimp factory at close quarters. The chicks were almost as big as their parents, with down the colour of the Cape's volcanic gravel and basalt. They were grouped into large squawking crèches, and would gang up in twos or threes to harass, and even chase, the feeding mothers. We could have watched them for days on end.

The hut held many mementoes of Shackleton's expedition, although it had something of a curated feel to it. It was built of Baltic pine, bleached and much abraded by wind and snow, and nestled into the rounded low hillocks of the Cape. Along one face, bits and pieces of a motor car rusted amid the remains of a garage made of boxes.

We had a meal and a few drinks that night with the two friendly New Zealanders who were stationed at the Cape to measure the deformation of the beaches in order to determine the extent of the ice sheet during the last glaciation. Next morning Nigel was up early to paint the penguins. Snow was driving in and the temperature had dropped. As in the Taylor Valley, he painted on the ground, canvas weighed down with stones, oblivious to the drift.

The helicopter from RNZAF3 Squadron picked us up late in the morning and dropped us down at Cape Evans, about eleven kilometres south of Cape Royds. We spent five hours at this most famous site in the Antarctic – Captain Scott's base for his last expedition. Cape Evans is by far the most interesting and poignant of the historic sites on Ross Island. The hut sits near one end of North Bay, a long surf beach of black volcanic gravel. In high summer the coast here can be quite open and, for the first time on our trip, we heard the crash of waves and the rattling of shingle. To the north lay the cliffs of the Barne Glacier where it meets McMurdo Sound. Looking south, we saw scattered islands: Inaccessible Island, Tent Island, Big and Little Razorback Islands. Further south, the Erebus Glacier Tongue stretched out into Erebus Bay.

The hut itself was a plain structure, long and low, with a simple gabled roof. Lean-to additions on two sides served as stables, storerooms and entrance porch. The elements have worn away the cladding of the hut, and the boxes of stores piled against its walls, to the colour of old bone. Debris lay everywhere: broken bottles with the ferrous green colour of Edwardian common glass; half-open boxes, their contents spilled out and scattered; clusters of cases and gear on the slopes behind the hut; the skeleton of a dog still chained to a post.

Shackleton's Hut, Cape Royds: (left to right) Bill Manhire, Chris Orsman, Nigel Brown.

As Tim unlocked the door of the hut we all felt mixed emotions and a mild sense of ceremony, as if we were approaching an inner sanctuary or a tomb. Shackleton's hut at Cape Royds had been clean, warm-toned, slightly sterile, the kind of place you could easily imagine yourself settling in for the night. It was as if the occupants had simply taken themselves off, leaving the place to newcomers. Nothing of them lingered there much. Scott's hut was different. In its own modest way it was like a tomb of the Pharaohs, where everything necessary for their life, their favourite and familiar things, had been gathered around them for the journey to the underworld. We saw their books, their darned socks and hot water bottles, their bunks and sealskin sleeping-bags, their beakers and retorts, their pipe racks, pinned calendars and magazine cut-outs. There was food here for the journey, too: boxes of Colman's flour and Fry's cocoa; shelves of bottled salt and pickle jars, some still in their straw wrappings; there were soups and consommés in abundance; and tin after tin of preserved meats: tongue, quail, rabbit, beef, pork. But it was food for the dead, grave food, mummy wheat.

The intactness of it all was astonishing, despite the dilapidations. I recalled Ponting's crisp photographs of the hut and its occupants from the books I read as a child in my grandparent's glory room. I matched them in my mind to the present scene and found an uncanny, rather ghostly fit, as eloquent in its absences as its presences.

As we walked around, looking into sleeping alcoves, the darkroom, the scientists' quarters, shining torches into the pantries, glancing at the magazines and newspapers, we all felt a little of what you feel at an open home: sanctioned yet trespassing. Later, when the rest of the party were outside exploring the surroundings, I slipped back inside and spent half an hour at Scott's desk. It was covered in black Formica, with various objects lying around: ashtrays, tins, a copy of Browning's verse, a stuffed penguin. A copy of the *Illustrated London News* also lay there, dated February 1910. I read it quietly for a time. I remember some pen drawings on the cover called 'Mannerisms of the Member', obviously a series on British Parliamentarians. The minister gesturing in the drawings was not unlike myself in physical appearance: balding, in his early forties, wearing spats and a stiff collar and a suit that must have been well in fashion. I had a strange sense of time opening up like a wound, aching at the consciousness of what had passed by irrevocably. Yet the detritus of that age was still preserved intact at Cape Evans. This long-dead British MP was a symbol of it all: archaic, hopelessly dated, and yet true to his age – like the hut, like the shelved goods, like Scott and his men. As I went out into the sunlight of the Cape I had the distinct feeling that the Captain himself had been there, whispering to my mind. I tried later to put something of the experience into a poem:

The Hut at Cape Evans

A bleached foreclosure
of what is rare in Antarctica:

walled, roofed space. You enter
through a smell of blubber,

harness oil, ponies.
Shelved tins everywhere

rust in profusion, labels
take colour a little

in the breathed-on light
from unshuttered windows.

Barley lies scattered on the stable floor,
the biscuit barrel's prised

to replenish the nibbling ghosts
who read over your shoulder.

We flew back to Scott Base early in the afternoon. It was bliss to be able to shave and shower and eat fresh food again. It was 'Boys' Night' on the menu, and Jeff the green-haired cook had prepared steak, chips and salad. We tucked in with gusto.

We still had plenty to do before we left Antarctica. We were planning to publish a small book of poems and had less than twenty-four hours in which to do it. I sat up until two o'clock in the morning in the computer room, typing up the poems I had cajoled out of Bill and Nigel. Bill was there for a time himself, translating his field notes into verse.

We completed our project the next day – a day of frantic activity, proofing, cutting, pasting, xeroxing and binding. Nigel carved a linocut for the cover of the book and printed up copies using a dessert spoon as a crude inker. We appropriated the TAE (Transantarctic Expedition hut) as our workplace. This 1950s hut is now a museum, filled with mementoes of early life at Scott Base. In Sir Edmund Hillary's office someone had thoughtfully draped a towel over the back of the chair. We used it liberally until we discovered that it was a museum piece, too, a souvenir of the great man.

That evening we put on a poetry reading and art exhibition in the dining room of Scott Base. It was well-attended, with visitors coming across from McMurdo Station and a party of RNZAF men from 3 Squadron. Afterwards, we presented copies of our book, *Homelight – an Antarctic Miscellany*, to the base manager, Ron Rogers.

Our last two days in Antarctica were pretty crammed. We made a couple of trips to McMurdo Station, about three kilometres away. Once off-base, the culture becomes quite American. Vehicles drive on the right-hand side; you end up with American dollars in your pockets; you hear American accents on the shuttle bus. McMurdo has been described as an Alaskan mining town in the Antarctic. There was certainly a functional ugliness about it, not entirely without charm. The buildings looked like huge insulated sheds with small entries. Everywhere there were power lines, bus sheds, Stop signs, and hitching posts with power points where you plugged in your vehicle to keep it heated in the sub-zero temperatures. We ate Sno-freeze and drank grape juice in the huge cafeteria, poked our noses into the busy hairdressing saloon, and wandered down to the most serene place in town, the little Chapel of the Snows on the shore. The chapel, sitting under its little steeple, was the only building in Antarctica that made a concession to something other than function. Inside, it was carpeted, warm and welcoming. We chatted for some time with the American pastor. I sat and prayed in the small alcove that held the reserved sacrament. Across the bay a red icebreaker of the US Coastguard was tied up to the wharf. Further along, a lonely hut stood out on a small headland appropriately named Hut Point. This was the Discovery hut, erected in 1901 for Scott's first expedition.

Friday was to be our last full day together. Nigel and I were due to fly out early on Saturday morning. Bill, as Poet Laureate, had been invited to the South Pole as a cultural ambassador. Tim was to accompany him, and they would fly home early next week. We had two pieces of filming to complete. One was a shot of the three artists walking out into the 'white expanse', which we filmed on the McMurdo Ice Shelf, taking the opportunity to ham it up a little.

The second task was more arduous – to climb Observation Hill (228 metres high) and read Tennyson's poem 'Ulysses' under the heavy jarrah cross erected to commemorate Scott and his four companions. It was a hard climb: the day was bitterly cold and we were wearing full survival gear. Once at the top, standing alongside the dark man-hauled cross, the panorama seemed to draw Antarctica into a unity for a brief moment of time. We could see small clusters of human habitation below us to the left and right: Scott Base and McMurdo Station. To the north and north-east stretched the sea ice; the ice-breakers had cut a long zigzag track through to the open water of the Sound. Further north lay the bite of Erebus Bay, the Glacier Tongue, and Cape Evans. Mt Erebus and the land eastwards were shrouded in snow drift. The Royal Society Range stood out in sharp relief to the west, the entrance to the Taylor Valley lost in a jumble of coastline. Due south, low islands marked the passage across the Ross Ice Shelf to the Pole.

I drew a crumpled xerox from my jacket and began to read Tennyson's poem, finishing with the famous line that was carved into the wood above my head: 'To strive, to seek, to find, and not to yield'.

Contributors' biographical notes

Catharina van Bohemen went to Zimbabwe in 1994 with her husband, Gerald Kember. They walked through parts of Chizarira and Kazuma Pan National Parks for two weeks. Between noon and about three, it was too hot to walk, and while the others in the group either read or slept, she began to write about being on safari. Living in Auckland with her husband and four children, van Bohemen teaches small children the recorder, writes, and is a regular reviewer for *The Evening Post*.

Joy Cowley has published adult novels and a collection of adult stories, as well as junior fiction and children's picture books. She travels widely, recently to Polynesia, Singapore, Malaysia and Brunei, and extensively throughout the United States. Much of her travel is in connection with her children's writing, which has been a major focus for the past fifteen years. She is recognised in the US as one of the leading contributors to reading programmes, with over 500 titles in print. Cowley has won awards for her books and her work is currently issued by some fifteen publishing houses. She lives with her husband in the Marlborough Sounds.

Tessa Duder's first big journey was aged six by sea to Britain, followed by an air journey at seventeen to represent New Zealand in swimming at the 1958 Empire Games in Cardiff. Since then, although a passionate Aucklander, she has spent periods living in London, Pakistan, Turangi and Malaysia, and as a writer has travelled in New Zealand, Australia, the US and Sweden. The engagement in 1995 of her third daughter to a Turkish carpet dealer, and subsequent arrival of a grandchild in 1997, began a happy association with Turkey and especially the tourist resort of Pamukkale. She has published seven novels for young people, as well as anthologies, histories, plays and short stories for both children and adults. She has four daughters and lives in Herne Bay, Auckland.

Contributors' biographical notes

Barbara Else runs the Wellington-based TFS Literary Agency with her husband Chris. She is the author of the novels *The Warrior Queen* and *Gingerbread Husbands*, which have been published both in New Zealand (by Godwit) and overseas, and of a children's book, *Skitterfoot Leaper*. A new novel, *Eating Peacocks* will be published later this year. Else has lived all over New Zealand and in California, and thoroughly enjoys travel – in retrospect.

Michaelanne Forster immigrated from California to New Zealand with her family in 1973. She writes television and radio scripts, plays, children's books and short stories. She was Writer-in-Residence at University of Canterbury in 1995, and has won a number of awards including Best Radio Drama (RNZ 1996 and 1997), and the Buckland Award for Literature for her play *Daughters of Heaven*. Her first non-fiction book, *When It's Over: New Zealanders talk about their experiences of separation and divorce* – has recently been published by Penguin.

Lloyd Jones is a Wellington-based writer married to an American with whom he has three children. He is the author of several books, including *Swimming to Australia* (a short story collection), *Biografi, This House Has Three Walls*, and the novel *Choo Woo*, which will be published in mid-1998. Also a journalist, he has published many travel articles in overseas newspapers and journals.

Graeme Lay was born in Foxton, raised in Taranaki and educated at Victoria University. He began writing in the mid-1970s. He is the author of two collections of short stories, two novels and two works of non-fiction including the travel book, *Passages: Journeys in Polynesia*. He also edited the collections *100 New Zealand Short Short Stories* and *Another 100 New Zealand Short Short Stories*. His most recent work is the young adult novel, *Leaving One-Foot Island* (Mallinson Rendel, 1998).

Joy MacKenzie is an Auckland poet, freelance writer, reviewer and tutor of ESL and creative writing. She won the *Sunday Star* short-story competition in 1991, was finalist in the 1992 Reed Fiction Award and received the Lilian Ida Smith Award in 1994. Her poems and stories have been published in literary magazines and been broadcast on radio. Her two most recent ambitions are to finish her novel and to return to Paris.

Chris Orsman was born in 1955 in Lower Hutt and lives and writes in Wellington. He has published three collections of verse, *Ornamental Gorse* (VUP, 1994), *South: an Antarctic Journey* (VUP, 1996) and *Black South* (Pemmican Press, 1997). His collection *South* will be published in the UK in 1999 by Faber & Faber.

Sarah Quigley has spent the past five years living in England and America, but returned to Auckland to take up the Buddle Findlay Sargeson Fellowship early in 1998. Her short story collection *having words with you* was published by Penguin, for whom she is now working on a novel. Her fiction and poetry have been published in various magazines and anthologies, and she is currently fiction editor for *Takahe*.

CK Stead, born in 1932 in Auckland, has published ten books of poems, seven novels, two collections of short stories, and four books of literary criticism, and has edited several anthologies. His most recent books are *Straw into Gold* (poems), and *The Blind Blonde with Candles in her Hair* (stories). He is married with three children and several grandchildren.

Peter Wells left New Zealand to study social history at the University of Warwick, where Germaine Greer had taught. He stayed in Britain five years and came home relatively unwillingly in the last years of Muldoon. Since then he has lived through the rapid social and economic changes with an increasing sense of disbelief. In between times he makes films (*Desperate Remedies*) and writes fiction (*Boy Overboard*).